AN AMERICAN FAMILY IN ITALY:

Living La Dolce Vita without Permission

Paul R. Spadoni

In memory of our good friends Steve and Patti Gray,

who helped and inspired me beyond description.

And they still do.

Table of Contents

Chapter 1: Il sogno begins 1

Chapter 2: Real Italian cousins 7

Chapter 3: An offer I can't refuse 13

Chapter 4: Committed! 19

Chapter 5: Final preparations 29

Chapter 6: Uno straniero in paradiso 31

Chapter 7: Reunited in a new land... 43

Chapter 8: Teaching for the Godfather 47

Chapter 9: Meeting, eating, Italian style............................... 53

Chapter 10: Adjustment agonies.. 61

Chapter 11: Chasing the permesso di soggiorno 67

Chapter 12: Finding our way... 75

Chapter 13: Making friends.. 85

Chapter 14: Settling in at school 91

Chapter 14: Adventures and misadventures......................... 95

Chapter 15: Blundering along with good humor.................. 107

Chapter 16: Wine, women and aggressive males 113

Chapter 17: Freedom to explore Italian roots 123

Chapter 18: Becoming more Italian 129

Chapter 19: Conflicts at home.. 135

Chapter 20: Scope for the imagination 139

Chapter 21: Cultural observations 143

Chapter 22: Making progress.. 155

Chapter 23: Making ends meet 163

Chapter 24: An end that is actually a beginning.................. 167

Postscript: Chasing the elusive magical elf called Permesso di Soggiorno.. 175

Grazie... 182

An interview with Paul Spadoni.. 183

Chapter 1: Il sogno begins

I never planned to be an illegal alien—but I was desperate. I was about to move to Italy for a year, and time had run out to get permission to live there legally. I'd tried to get my Italian citizenship, but my blundering efforts to overcome Italian bureaucracy utterly failed. I'd looked for an employer who would help me get a work permit—with no success. I'd already bought non-refundable flight tickets for my family of four and committed to taking a one-year leave of absence from my teaching job in the United States. So, when I received a job offer with cash payments, no visa requirements and no work permit, I jumped on it like a man who had just downed a quadruple espresso.

Why was I so determined to move to Italy? Wearing a cheap fedora and impersonating an Italian cousin in Venice had sparked this life-changing decision.

I was forty-three at the time, teaching journalism, photography and graphic design at Peninsula High School in Gig Harbor, Washington. My daughter Sandy, age seventeen and a junior at Peninsula, was finishing a one-year stay in Poland as part of a Rotary Club exchange program. She and another American student wanted to do some traveling around Europe, including Italy, before returning.

It had been challenging enough for us to let our little girl live with strangers halfway around the world—*but now she wanted to backpack Europe with another teenage girl and no adult supervision?* Wasn't Italy the place where males pinched foreign girls on their bottoms? Isn't there a famous photo of Italian guys leering at an American woman? Sandy had asked our permission, reassuring us that she and a friend were now experienced and mature travelers, and they would support each other. They had already spent the money to get to Poland, and it would be a shame not to see some of the rest of Europe as well, she pleaded. We told Sandy we would think about it and get back to her.

"It's obvious what we need to do," my wife, Lucy, said.

"Yes, she'll be disappointed," I replied, "but at least she'll be safe."

"No, I'm not saying she shouldn't go. She should. But *you* should go with her; you should be her escort. You've always dreamed of going to Italy and meeting your relatives, and this would be a perfect time."

"That's crazy! No way can I drop everything and go to Italy. I've got too many responsibilities. I can't just leave everything and fly away."

"Sure you can," she countered. "Sandy won't be in Italy for another twenty days. You'll have time to get ready."

"Listen, I'd have to miss the last three days of school. How am I going to get a substitute? I'll have tests and projects to grade. Anyway, I don't even have a passport, and I think it takes six weeks to get one."

"But you've wanted to go to Italy since you were in high school. Your parents wanted to give you a trip to Europe as a college graduation present, remember? You've been studying Italian on your own the past two years. You have to do this!"

Lucy remembered that I had skipped out on the free European tour for some crazy reason—wanting to marry her as soon as possible after college. Maybe she felt bad that I had traded that trip in for much needed cash. But Lucy's a determined woman, and she set her mind to make this happen. She found out how to get an expedited passport and set me up with an appointment. Then she helped me find a substitute. She made reservations at a hostel and even packed my suitcases while I worked feverishly to finish grading and write instructions for the substitute. Thinking back, the preparations are still a blur. Maybe that's because I didn't make any.

As hurried as we were, though, we did take the time to develop a devious prank. We told Sandy to go to a hostel in the Guidecca area of Venezia; there she would be met by cousin Pietro Spadoni, and he would escort her around Italy. I didn't even know if we had a cousin Pietro; the plan was for me to pretend to be Sandy's Italian cousin. She wasn't convinced she needed an escort, but we insisted and she agreed. She and her buddy took a train from Hungary that passed through Croatia and Slovenia and arrived in Venezia together, where they spent a couple of days. Her friend departed to go to France, Spain and Portugal while Sandy waited to meet her "cousin." In the twenty days since Lucy and I had cooked up this plan, I had grown a mustache, Lucy had bought me a fedora (I never wore hats) and I practiced my fake Italian accent.

I had never traveled to Europe before, and I exited the airport gate dazed, only to be greeted by a cacophony of aggressive *uomini* offering me taxi rides, hotels or to take me by water taxi to my destination. I took a deep breath, shook my head at every offer and asked at the information desk how to get into Venice. The agent recommended I take a blue bus. Knowing nothing about the city, I wondered how a bus could carry me to an island, but it turns out there is a bridge. Once there, the sights, the smells and the sounds of diverse tongues assailed my senses. African merchants had spread colorful merchandise on the sidewalks, and I stared for a full minute at a little cardboard Mickey Mouse bouncing on stringy legs to the music of a boom box. Snapping out of a trance, I asked at the *punto informazioni* how to get to the Ostello Venezia, bought a ticket for the *vaporetto,* wrestled my suitcases aboard and found out where to exit. I asked the pilot to alert me when we were coming to the Guidecca stop, and then I stuck close to him while nervously reading the names at every dock, just in case he forgot me. I listened in on Italian conversations and despaired at how few words I could understand. Despite my sense of having landed on another planet, I arrived without problems and checked in several hours before Sandy and I were to meet. I explored some quiet side streets and returned. And then, there she was, standing in the lobby!

"*Buon giorno,*" I greeted her heartily. "You must-a be Sandra Spadoni. I am-a you *cugino*, Pietro."

"Wow!" she gasped, staggering backward and shaking her head. "You look so much like my dad! I can't believe it. The resemblance is *amazing!*"

"He must-a be one helluva *bell'uomo,*" I replied.

Unfortunately, that's actually not what she said at all. That's how the conversation went in my imagination; it's how it should have gone. Instead, she recognized me immediately.

"Dad? DAD! What are you doing here?"

"*No, no, non sono tuo padre.* I am-a Pietro, *tuo cugino.*"

"No, you're my dad, and where did you get that silly hat? And what's with the mustache?"

I had to give up. My disappointment at having failed to fool her couldn't match our joy at being reunited after nearly a year, and we had two weeks to plan together in a land of dreams.

While enjoying triple cones of stracciatella, tiramisú and fragola at a *gelateria* overlooking the Grand Canal, I asked Sandy if I hadn't fooled her for just a second.

"Come on, you're my one and only papa. I should hope I could always recognize you, even in a fedora and a patchy mustache. But it was a shock! I think that was your best practical joke ever, even though you didn't trick me.

The magic of Venezia so overcame me that I quickly forgave her for calling my mustache patchy when I distinctly remember it as a thick, full bush of pure manliness.

We spent a day in Venezia before going to Firenze and then Montecatini, where we met many cousins, including, to our surprise, the real Pietro Spadoni. He did look a little like me, but without the amazing mustache and fedora. As it turned out, no one in Italy actually wears a fedora.

Chapter 2: Real Italian cousins

To save money, we ended up taking a slow train in the middle of the night from Venezia to Firenze. It arrived about 5 a.m., and as no trains departed for our cousins' smaller station of Montecatini until later in the morning, we had to hang out in the chilly early hours with no place to go. At around 7 a.m., we saw people running to get in line for something, so we followed them and got in line too. It turned out to be for the Uffizi Gallery, one of the oldest and most famous art museums in the world. We paid the entry fee and went inside to look at works by Giotto, Botticelli, da Vinci, Raffaello, Michelangelo, Caravaggio, Tiziano and other renowned artists. We became separated for quite a long time as we wandered around. Amazed as we should have been by these works of genius, we both fell asleep in different rooms because of our exhausting overnight trip and frigid early morning wait outside.

After our impromptu naps, we continued to Montecatini and spent a good part of a week at the home of second cousin Enrico Spadoni and his wife Enza, along with their children Alessandra and Simone. Alessandra spoke some English, but the adults none at all. At first, I thought thirteen-year-old Simone spoke English well, as he immediately engaged me in conversation, asking me about my family, my hobbies and my taste in music. Then he fell silent, and I realized he had used up all his English in fewer than three minutes. So I asked him what he was studying in school and his favorite sports and music—and then, for the same reason, I fell silent as well. So much for language lessons!

We were treated to banquet after banquet of exquisite home-cooked meals starting with an antipasto and proceeding to risotto, pasta asciutta, lasagne, bistecca, various vegetables and always a dolce with sweet wine and ending with espresso. We also dined like royalty with Enrico's brother Loriano and his family. Alessandra took us on a personal tour of landmarks in Firenze—the Duomo, Ponte Vecchio, the church of Dante and Beatrice and other landmarks that we knew were important historical sites but meant almost nothing to us because of our glaring lack of knowledge about Italian history, art and literature. Enrico took us on a private tour of a Medici fortress, memorable more for the fact that we were together with our cousin than for the site's historical significance. It didn't help that we couldn't understand the Italian guide.

Gianfranco, the husband of Marta, another second cousin, drove us around the local countryside. He showed us a parking lot in San Salvatore and explained that the house of my *nonno* had once stood there. It had been torn down to make a *piazza* around 1970. Gianfranco was the only cousin who spoke English well, and he helped me translate a little speech I had written that I wanted to read to my relatives. It went like this: "My family instilled pride in me at an early age in being Italian and in all things that are Italian. Because of this, I have always wanted to come here, not just to see the famous sights, but to understand what it is like to live as an Italian. Someday I hope to return not just for a visit but to live here long enough to really understand the day-to-day lifestyle of the people. Thank you so much for your hospitality and for sharing your lives with us."

It was the first time I had expressed aloud a wish to return to Italy for a more extended encounter. Saying it in Italian somehow made the desire more real. My cousins seemed touched by my sincere sentiments, though I do recall Enrico expressing disbelief that someone from a country where life seemed predictable and logical would want to submit to the frustrating inefficiencies of life in Italy. While he didn't come right out and say it, I suspect he wanted to ask if I was crazy—a question I would eventually ask myself.

We met many more relatives, taking a day trip to Pisa to see the famous leaning *torre* and meet another cousin there. We also attended a yard party to celebrate the first communion of a young relative. It reminded me of our Spadoni family annual Fourth of July parties, although with my limited Italian, I really didn't get to talk to anyone in the short time we were there. Standing in the midst of this torrent of Babble, I wondered if my Italian relatives could tell me more about how long the Spadoni family had lived in this area. They knew their grandparents but almost nothing about our shared great grandparents Pietro Spadoni and Maria Marchi. Where did Pietro live before he moved to San Salvatore, which was only about five minutes from where we stood? Did he have brothers and sisters? What did he do for a living? Presumably he was a farmer, like his children, but all in all, these Italian cousins showed a singular lack of curiosity about genealogy and family history.

I didn't understand this. Growing up American but surrounded by my Italian-American cousins, I felt a strong connection to the home of my ancestors and pride in my heritage. My grandparents were the first Italians to settle in Gig Harbor, and their seven children all built houses within a few miles of the original family home. My grandmother's three siblings all settled in Gig Harbor, and so did two of my grandfather's nephews. We had family gatherings every Fourth of July, Christmas Eve and Christmas morning. We were the Little Italy of the town, and everyone knew everyone. Now I was in Italy, and I wanted to dig more deeply into our roots, but that didn't appear possible.

Alex Haley, the author of *Roots*, wrote: "In all of us, there is a hunger, bone-marrow deep, to know our heritage—to know who we are and where we have come from. Without this enriching knowledge, there is a hollow yearning. No matter what our attainments in life, there is still a vacuum, an emptiness, and the most disquieting loneliness."

While I related perfectly well with Haley's conviction, my Italian cousins seemed immune to this hunger of the marrow. Looking at the grandparents at the yard party, it slowly dawned on me that these people already knew where they came from. Italian families typically stay in the same region for centuries, sometimes millennia, so my Italian relatives understood their roots in a way that we Italian-Americans can't comprehend. I still yearned to know what my ancestors' lives had been like, and what they had given up to start new lives in America, but my cousins lived their cultural history every day. People of the older generation had lived their lives in a way not much removed from that of their own grandparents—and of their ancestors of a thousand years before, for that matter.

I also realized that one can keep up with only a limited number of cousins at one time. Because my grandfather and grandmother had moved to America in the early 1900s, my American relatives were either uncles or first and second cousins, so I knew nearly 100 percent of my kin. Meanwhile, my Italian relatives realized they were surrounded by innumerable distant cousins, and who has time to maintain close relationships with 700 people? That would make for one riotous, unmanageable Christmas party. Ah, but think of the heavenly food that would be served!

Sandy and I continued on to visit the Vatican, Rome and Milan. We took a long ferry ride on Lake Como, from Lecco to Bellagio and back. By the end of our trip, I was convinced that Sandy could take care of herself and would be safe traveling in Europe, so she went on to explore Paris and England before returning.

The trip awakened in me the realization that I was approaching a new stage in my life, and that fresh possibilities were around the corner. Lucy and I have four children. The year before, our eldest son Randy had graduated from high school, and now Sandy would do the same in just a year. Taking a wife and four kids to Italy would have been too difficult, but with only two teenagers—Suzye and Lindsey—left at home, I could see us all jumping on a plane bound for *la dolce vita*—I could see it so clearly that I kicked off plans to make it happen.

Chapter 3: An offer I can't refuse

Lucy said she supported my dream, but was she just being polite? Would she really be willing to pack up and move our family overseas? One thing is certain about my wife: She may be the most honest and transparent person alive. She's never been able to mask her emotions or hold back her opinions. She's not even good at telling jokes, because the best anecdotes involve a hint of deception so as not to reveal any clues that could betray the punchline, and deception is just not in her nature. She said she was on board all the way, and so I believed her. Over the next few years, I continued my on-again off-again study of Italian. We also hosted two exchange students from Italy, first Simone and then Silvia. Actual Italian classes were hard to find in Gig Harbor. Sometimes in nearby Tacoma a kind of Italian-for-travelers class was offered, but more complete lessons were an hour away in Seattle. We both tried taking the Seattle classes for a session, but two hours of driving and two hours of class time twice a week exhausted me after having put in a full day of work.

I bought a book about living and working in Italy, which both raised and dashed my hopes at the same time. Of all the professions, teaching is one of the most transferable from one country to another. Italy has quite a few American and British schools for children of expatriates and Italians who want their children to be bilingual. This sounded promising—but everything I found out after that hopeful point looked gloomy.

One of my colleagues, Jack, had found a teaching job in Saudi Arabia along with his wife.

"How does one go about getting an overseas job? I asked him.

"You'll need to go to conferences with International School Services, where recruiters come from overseas schools to hire teachers," he said. "And you'll need to make at least a two-year overseas commitment."

"Can't do that," I replied. "My daughters would freak out to leave their friends for that long, and I can't get a two-year leave of absence from the school district. I love my job and want it to be there when I come back."

"Also," Jack continued, "the schools overseas are looking for either unmarried teachers or husband-wife teaching teams, because they're a better deal financially for them. It's not a plus for applicants to have children, because the schools are usually obliged to provide free tuition."

Maybe, he added, some really remote schools in unattractive locations would be desperate enough to hire someone like me.

"So, where overseas do you want to teach?" he asked. "Hopefully somewhere where nobody wants to go?"

"Yeah, I'm sure I'll be the only one who's ever thought about living and working in Italy," I replied, with a mixture of sarcasm and despair. This would not be easy.

My research also raised doubts about whether I could ever obtain a work permit without first securing a job. The way it is supposed to work is you find a job in Italy—or better yet, you work for an American company that has branches in Italy—and the company verifies that the job requires skills that only a foreigner can provide and then helps you obtain a work permit. This process can take from four to twelve months, and companies don't relish the extra paperwork and waiting time. Italy is famous for art, food, architecture—and bureaucracy. I had my doubts that a company or school would go to much trouble for a new employee who only wanted to stay for a year.

But I refused to give up, and I used the Internet to find the names and addresses of every major American and British school in Italy and sent them all cover letters and résumés. I received no reply except one from a school near Firenze, which sent a form postcard stating, among other things, that they received approximately 3,000 inquiries per year and they only hired through agencies such as ISS. I imagined that the other schools would have said the same thing, if they had been willing to waste the postage to reply.

Another possibility was teaching at a Department of Defense Dependents school, but that looked even less promising. I would have to take a PRAXIS exam to provide a measurement of my skills and knowledge, fill out lengthy forms and obtain letters of recommendation. The application form and letters would have to be repeated each year. I read that one applicant received a form rejection letter stating that 7,000 people applied for 300 jobs. Additionally, teachers can't choose where they will be assigned. While there are American military bases in Italy, most of the teachers there started in less desirable countries and then transferred to Italy when an opening occurred. Even with all these factors against me, I did give DODDS a try at one stage in the late 1990s. Alas, I heard nothing back, and I gave up on this impossible long shot.

Yet my research didn't completely dash my hopes. I read that it's possible to find short-term jobs in language institutes where the employers don't always concern themselves with all the troublesome legalities such as work permits and visas. Further, these jobs were said to be fairly plentiful and easy to obtain for an English speaker with a background in education. The chief drawback was that such jobs are low paying, and they can't be secured from abroad. One has to actually go to Italy and show up on the doorstep to be offered a job.

I started regularly checking the website wantedinrome.com, which had classified ad sections that showed both housing prices and jobs available for English speakers. The housing was expensive, but I knew that the cost of living outside Rome would not be as steep. Most encouragingly, I was struck by the fact that there always seemed to be a half dozen or more ads from language institutes looking for mother-tongue English teachers. While some required training or experience in teaching English as a second language, others offered on-the-job training. With twenty-plus years teaching high school English, I had no doubt I could find a job—in Rome, at least. It was not my first choice of cities—it was too big, too international for me—but I would take it.

The bigger questions that remained were whether I could come anywhere close to supporting a family on one of these jobs, and would they really give me a job without a work permit or obtain one for me? The last question seemed easy enough to answer, since all of the language schools had e-mail addresses. I wrote about ten of them, asking about salaries, training and work permits, but not a single one wrote back. After a month of waiting, I decided to make some phone calls. The results were discouraging.

"Would you hire someone with twenty years of experience teaching English but no experience teaching English as a foreign language?"

"Perhaps. Make an appointment and bring in your curriculum vitae."

"I'm not coming to Italy until September. Do you usually have openings then?"

"Sometimes. It depends. Come and visit us then, and we'll see."

"Can you hire an American without a work permit, or would you help an American get a work permit?"

This question elicited various vague answers. I only received one outright refusal. One respondent said there seemed to be many Americans teaching English, so it must somehow be possible. Others said they didn't know, but I could come in and talk to the director about it. Reading between the lines, I realized that some of the agencies would hire me without a work permit if I came to the door ready to work and had a decent résumé, but they were loathe to state this over the phone. None of them wanted to declare to a complete stranger that they didn't follow the law. Also, this is not the type of industry that hires in advance. Language teachers are somewhat transient and are both in demand and yet plentiful. Since the pay and benefits are low, one doesn't find many people making advance arrangements for this type of job. More often, someone without definite plans or responsibilities may come to Italy, decide they want to stay and then look around for an entry level job—which they can find in a language institute.

Slowly a plan began to form. I would apply for a leave of absence, which had to happen nearly a year in advance. I could cancel the request a little past mid-year if I got cold feet. Then I would send out another round of letters to British and

American schools. If I didn't get a conventional teaching job, I would try a language institute as backup.

Once again I heard nothing from the foreign schools. February was approaching, and with it the deadline for withdrawing my leave request.

"What are we going to do?" I asked Lucy. "A job at a language institute *might* support a single person, but no way a family of four. I'll need to let the school district know in a few weeks if I want to withdraw my leave of absence."

"I think God wants us to go," she said. "He's put this desire in your heart for a reason. He'll find a way for us to make it."

"I'm not going there to be a missionary," I countered. "Why does God care if I spend a year in Italy teaching at a foreign school?"

"Maybe there's some other reason," she said. "We just need to trust that this will work out if we keep doing all that we can. I think it was meant to be."

I realized that if I waited until I had a sure job before committing to Italy, I would never make it. If we took out a home equity line of credit and we had a good summer with my side job, our family-run asphalt maintenance business, we could probably survive a year in Italy even with a low paying job. Lucy had recently taken classes in ESL instruction— English as a second language—and she could also get a job, if necessary.

We decided to go for it.

I let the deadline for withdrawing my leave request pass by.

Chapter 4: Committed!

In March, we took another semi-irreversible step. I purchased non-refundable discount airfare tickets to Italy for our family, and I announced to my colleagues at Peninsula High School that we were moving to Italy for a year.

Reactions from my colleagues ranged from amazement to envy, usually both at once. I was flooded with logical questions: "What city? Where will you live? What's your job going to be? Will you be able to earn enough to meet expenses? Do you have friends there to help you make the transition? Do you speak Italian?" Most people knew me as a quiet, conservative and methodical person who had taught at the same school for twenty years. I could see looks of bafflement and almost shock when I told them I had no good answers to any of these questions, but I was going nevertheless. I think people were too polite to tell me they thought I was crazy, but I'm sure the thought occurred to them.

"Well, we're committed now," Lucy said.

"Yes, well, some people think we should be committed somewhere else," I answered.

A few years prior, a longtime teacher at the school abruptly left her job to join a fringe "end-of-the-world is nigh" cult in Montana. Her friends tried to talk her out of it, but she left anyway. I think some people wondered if I was going the same way.

"You know, it would be a lot easier just to go out and buy a red sports car in America if you're having a mid-life crisis," joked one of my colleagues. "But since you're determined to go, be sure to bring me back a red Ferrari Testosterone, or whatever they call those things."

Why would I leave a secure job heading a successful journalism program to search for a temporary job in a foreign country? Didn't I have home and car payments to meet, college loans for my older children, credit cards debts and other assorted obligations to meet? Simply packing up and moving overseas to a new job would be a big step, most people thought—to move overseas with no job was stupefying. Perhaps it should have been for us as well.

I couldn't come right out and say it, but deep inside I agreed that Lucy had a point when she said that our plans were meant to be. I'm not sure how to explain it, but I felt it was my destiny to go to Italy. Some people refer to this feeling as a calling, but that didn't feel right to me. Called, in the religious sense of the word, didn't fit. True, a call would be consistent with my Christian beliefs, but a call seems to fit better when it involves a spiritual vocation. I didn't feel called to be a missionary to Italy, just to *be* in Italy. We both had the feeling that I would somehow find a job. Lucy said that if I thought I needed to go to Italy, then it was her destiny too. She was all in. *Santa donna!*

Daughters Suzye and Lindsey, though, were another story entirely. Suzye was already in the midst of a mildly rebellious teenage phase, and Lindsey appeared poised to follow in her footsteps. They would hang out with their friends, talking and laughing for hours—and then speak to their parents in monosyllable one-word sentences. They were going to miss their junior and freshman years of high school for their dad's crazy dream, and they weren't happy about leaving their friends and busy social life—but they didn't want to talk about. Their main questions to me were, "Will we be able to instant message our friends in America?" and "When will we come home again?"

Whenever another adult questioned them on the subject, they would give curt, almost detached, replies. We had my sister Linda over for dinner one evening, and she tried to engage them.

"You girls are so lucky," Linda said to Suzye. "You'll have a great time. You must be really excited."

"Yeah, sure," Suzye said, without any enthusiasm.

"What do you think, Lindsey?"

"Ah, it'll be okay."

End of conversation.

Suzye—fair-haired, sensitive, emotional and usually perky and cheerful—had been fighting us on issues such as her under-performance in school, curfew, boyfriend, cigarettes, parties and attendance at punk rock concerts. Our family had always been close, loving and trusting, but Suzye was testing her limits and, we thought, trying to push into adulthood too quickly. Our decision to go to Italy came at a low point in our parent-child relationship.

My tool shop is not far from Suzye's bedroom, and one day I overheard a conversation between Suzye and Lindsey and one of their friends.

"I can't *believe* your parents are making you go to Italy," the friend said. "Won't they let you stay here and live with someone else?"

"Maybe," Suzye said. "I'm planning to ask them if I can live with Jessica."

"It doesn't seem real to me," Lindsey said. "It might be fun, but I can't get into it. I just don't know what it's going to be like. But I hate the thought of missing out on all the fun here."

"It really sucks," Suzye said. "I have a boyfriend and all of my friends, and we just have to leave them behind? They're all gonna be going to concerts and parties and hanging out, and we'll miss it all. I cried about it for hours last night."

Suzye did ask us about living with Jessica, but we quickly quashed that idea. Suzye was already abusing the freedom we were giving her. She had to accept the inevitable, but she still begged us to let her stay.

"Dad, please," she cried. "High school years are the best years of our lives. I'm gonna miss out on a quarter of my best times."

We tried to get Suzye and Lindsey interested in learning some Italian words and phrases, but they wanted nothing to do with it. "I'll learn it on the plane," Suzye said flippantly.

Lindsey modeled Suzye, who was her best friend. Being two years younger, she hadn't yet started testing her limits in the same ways as Suzye—but only because Lindsey and her same-age friends couldn't yet drive. Suzye was usually polite, quiet and submissive when talking to us directly, but Lindsey had a bolder and less openly emotional side. Suzye often prodded Lindsey to ask us for permission to take them places.

When Suzye came in after curfew, she quietly listened to our lectures and pleas and accepted the consequences without arguing. Lindsey, instead, asked me, "Dad, how I am going to learn things for myself if you don't let me make mistakes?"

She also focused so intently on what she was doing at every moment that she often misplaced jackets, books and other items because of lack of attention to these things. These moments of absent-mindedness made her seem like an airhead at times, but she was actually very intelligent, and she excelled in her classes.

In elementary school, Suzye and Lindsey had each read 100 books in the Tacoma library's summer reading club, making them eligible to receive an award from the mayor at a special meeting at the city hall. While waiting in line, Suzye concocted a mischievous scheme. When their turn came to shake hands with the mayor and receive their award certificates, they would each say something funny.

Lindsey's instructions were to paraphrase, in a heavy southern accent, a line that Forrest Gump had said to his bus driver on the first day of school: "My mamma told me not to shake hands with strangers." Suzye, next in the queue, would say: "Well, brass my buttons, which one's the mayor?"

Lindsey, the bold follower, delivered her lines to perfection, although her drawl made it a little hard to determine what she said. The mayor, surprised and impressed that someone actually spoke to him, said, "Well, I'm going to have to ask you to repeat that," and he held his microphone low so everyone could hear her say it again. Lucy and I looked at each other in shock and disbelief. Suzye giggled, shook hands with the mayor, and took her award without saying a word.

Now those innocent childhood memories and personality traits had transformed into something more serious. Suzye was leading Lindsey in more dangerous directions.

Perhaps the lowest point in our relationship came when I passed by Suzye's bedroom door and heard Lindsey say: "This crap isn't working. I don't feel at all high."

They had sent away for mail order drugs, paid for by the money they made working for me in our summer business. They had it delivered to the home of Jessica, the friend that Suzye had wanted to live with. Busted!

"They're not drugs," Lindsey countered. "They're all legal. They're just herbs and seeds and stuff like that."

I checked the website where they had ordered them. It was true—they were things like salvia (sage) and other plants I had never heard of, and their use was not regulated or restricted. However, a quick check on the website where the girls had found them revealed fantastic and specific claims for their "mood-enhancing" effects. Luckily, they had just unwrapped the order and only tried one sample, which had disappointed them for its lack of results.

I cautioned them about the dangers of taking untested and unregulated substances, but I was also slightly relieved to know that they weren't buying illegal narcotics from their friends. Or were they? No, of course they wouldn't do that, they said, but this purchase certainly didn't inspire my confidence in their decision-making skills. And it confirmed our conviction that we shouldn't let them stay in Gig Harbor with their friends.

We made plans for their schooling through a variety of means, signing them up for on-line and correspondence classes, and I developed a curriculum for an independent social studies class I called "Renaissance History," which my principal and a school counselor approved. We would read three books together, discuss them and take field trips to art museums. The girls would also take language classes in Italy, and we would apply for credit at their schools the following year back in Gig Harbor.

When I booked my flight in early spring, I scheduled it for the last week in August. I bought a second flight for Lucy and the girls to arrive ten days later, under an incredibly naive and mistaken notion that it would take me a week to find both a job and an apartment. But I still didn't give up on looking for a job while still in the states.

Schools try to do their hiring in the spring to have the first choice of the best candidates available. That also means administrators can go into the summer break with the assurance that they are fully staffed for the beginning of the next school year. But my years of involvement with education told me that school officials have to be ready for the unexpected. Almost every fall, life happens—someone resigns, takes a better job, gets pregnant, is fired, has a spouse who is transferred or something else unforeseen crops up—and administrators must scramble to find a replacement, sometimes even the day before school starts. Knowing this, I figured I could make phone calls in August to see if this might have happened at any of the schools on my list, but I also spent a little more postage to send out my résumé one more time. In my cover letter, I suggested that administrators post my résumé on their office bulletin board before they left for summer break so they could grab it when they came back to fill any sudden openings. I told them I was coming to Italy whether I had a job or not, so they wouldn't have to pay for my airfare or look far to find me.

In June, just before school let out for the summer, I received phone calls from two schools that already had unexpected openings. A school in Torino wanted me to have a work permit and wasn't sure I could get one before school started in the fall. I told them I was working on obtaining Italian citizenship, but I didn't think it would happen by the fall. They said they would keep me in mind but would continue to search for someone easier to hire.

The other school was in Padova—Padua in English—about half an hour west of Venice. It sounded like a long shot, because they were looking for an elementary school director. Why they would be interested in me, I had no idea, as I had absolutely no administrative experience or credentials. Well, that's not entirely true: I had been a department chairman for two years, but I had hated it. Teachers can be a complaining and whiny lot. True, students complain too, but in the classroom I usually didn't have to listen to griping if I didn't want to. I loved being a teacher and had no desire to be an administrator, yet if that's what it would take to work in Italy, I would do it. I told the school director, Dr. Gino Bianchi, to consider me as a candidate.

He suggested I call the nursery school director, to find out more details about what the job entailed. I called with the purpose of asking questions, but I ended up in the middle of a job interview, totally unprepared. She wanted to know about my philosophy of leadership and education. She asked questions about curriculum, programs and my ideas to improve the school. I do not speak fluent BS, which I consider an important skill for an administrator, so I floundered around trying to sound like I knew what I was doing. I'm sure that at the end of the conversation, both the nursery school director and I wondered what Dr. Bianchi could possibly have been thinking when he suggested I might be a candidate for this job.

A week later, Dr. Bianchi called again. Now he had a position open for a fifth grade instructor. Teachers at his school, the English International School of Padua, were hired on two-year contracts and stayed with the same students for both years. A teacher had left after only one year. I got the impression he had been very popular with the students but the parents didn't think his academic standards were strict enough. Gino, which I later learned everyone called Dr. Bianchi, wanted a teacher for just one year, and he wanted someone with a proven track record. My résumé looked good enough to him, and he also thought it would be nice if I could start a school newspaper and help with the school's website, areas in which I had lots of experience. We talked a bit about salary, housing and my family. He told me he could find an apartment for us and said Suzye and Lindsey could use computers at the school to do their on-line classes. He asked if I was interested in the job, and I told him to give me twenty-four hours to talk to my wife, but when I hung up the phone, I already knew we'd say yes.

Lucy seemed as excited as I about the job offer, but of course we had no other concrete options for comparison. I called Gino back the next day, asked a few more questions about salary, insurance and a work permit, and then I accepted enthusiastically.

Gino admitted the salary was not high. Teachers in Italy are generally poorly paid. Most of Gino's teachers were young, single women from England with few expenses, and he could get away with paying them even less than average because he also helped arrange housing for them. However, he said, in recognition that I had a family, he would pay me more, though I should not tell this to the other teachers to prevent jealousies. The higher salary turned out to be a half-truth—no, maybe only a quarter-truth, but I wouldn't find that out until my last week at the school. Even with the so-called higher salary, my pay would not cover our family's expenses. It was only about a third of what I received in America as a teacher at the top end of the pay scale—but we were going for the cultural experience, not to make a profit, and it was a step above teaching in a language institute.

But what about the work permit? "Really, we should get you a work permit," Gino said. "But they are difficult to get. There might not be enough time." He explained that I should claim that I was a tourist and not mention anything about work when I entered the country. He would pay me in cash. And though technically I should have a visa for such a long stay, nobody would actually check for these things. Our adventure as illegal aliens in Italy was about to begin!

Chapter 5: Final preparations

Now I didn't seem quite so crazy. I had a job, I would have an apartment and my daughters had a place to continue their schooling. We would have to work like crazy all summer to afford it and to get our house ready, but at least I knew where we were going. We put an ad in the newspaper and found a family that wanted to rent our house for ten months. Our summer road maintenance business was booming, and it kept all four of us steadily employed. Suzye and Lindsey were reliable and skilled workers, and they appreciated the above-average wages I paid them. I would send them out on one day to pressure wash asphalt driveways and parking lots, and then the next day we would all work together to apply two coats of sealer. Sometimes we would cut out sink holes and areas damaged by tree roots and repair the holes with hot asphalt. I kept the books, ran the advertising campaign, maintained the equipment and secured the jobs. Lucy drove our truck and trailer to Tacoma to fill the sealer tanks or haul asphalt, and she also re-striped any parking lots that we sealed. However, we also pushed the girls hard to help get the house ready during their spare time, and that added more strain to our relationships.

"Dad, we worked for you eight hours today, and now Mom wants me to help pack up the basement," Lindsey complained. "We need time with our friends, since we're not going to be able to see them all next year."

I also overreacted when I found out Suzye had stopped to visit with her boyfriend while I had sent her off to pressure wash a driveway. I assumed she expected to be paid for a full day of work despite a half hour boyfriend break, but she argued that she never intended to report having worked for the missed half hour when she filled out her time card.

That may have been true, but Suzye had lied to us on a few other occasions about her whereabouts. I had even gone out looking for her once when she was supposed to have been at a friend's house but wasn't. I saw Suzye and the friend in the back seat of a car in the driveway of a house notorious for teen parties, but they ducked down and the car sped away. Tension in our household reached an all-time high when I let Suzye know I had seen her in the car and that she would be grounded for a couple of weeks. Typical of Suzye, she didn't argue, but her once sunny disposition had turned melancholy, bordering on depression.

Lucy and Suzye were hardly talking at this point, and it seemed that we all needed a long vacation together . . . if only we could survive the preparations!

Chapter 6: Uno straniero in paradiso

One of my teaching colleagues had a late-summer gathering at her house just hours before I was to depart. At last I had concrete answers when I was asked about my trip to Italy. I would fly into Rome the next day and take a train to Padova, where I had a two-bedroom apartment and a job teaching fifth graders waiting for me. My family would join me in ten days.

"Keep your luggage with you on the train," advised the colleague. "You don't want it stolen." I remembered these words as I boarded the train at Fiumicino, the main airport that serves Rome. This was in the days when airlines didn't charge extra for luggage, and I had three very heavy suitcases, plus a substantial carry-on, which made it difficult to board the train. I had to leave two suitcases on the sidewalk while I grappled the first two aboard and hoped the last two would still be there when I returned for them. They were. I put them all in a luggage room, which was enclosed in glass, and I sat in a compartment right next to the room so I could keep an eye on my suitcases.

I struck up a conversation with two couples from Orlando, Florida. They were first-time visitors to the *bel paese* and had come to attend a wedding. They were typical middle-aged American tourists, friendly and talkative but with a touch of a superiority complex about our home country. They spent a good five minutes debating whether the train was or was not air conditioned while we all boiled in the sweltering frying pan that is Rome in August.

"Open the windows to let in some air," one woman told her husband.

"No, you don't open a window when the air conditioning is on," he said.

"Are you kidding? How can you say there's air conditioning when it's this hot?"

"Well, it's even hotter outside than it is in here."

He finally opened the window, but the results were inconclusive. They asked me about my trip and I explained my plans.

"Don't worry about your daughters," one of the men advised. "They'll thank you when they're in their twenties— that is, if they ever start speaking to you again."

When the train pulled into Rome's central station, I realized that I had neglected to keep an eye on my luggage. Happily, it was still there, but the Floridians weren't so fortunate. Someone had made off with a suitcase, which contained, among other things, a suit for the wedding. It could have been mine, I thought, although their sheer weight made my suitcases intimidating to filch. I had packed for a year, not two weeks, and my luggage had been carefully weighed to hold the absolute maximum allowable.

My many suitcases gave me one of my first opportunities to practice my shaky language skills. After standing next to an Italian-looking man on the crowded Rome-Bologna train for a couple of hours, I felt enough solidarity to ask for a favor as we pulled into the station. Unfortunately, I mixed up my verb cases, and my "Puó aiutarmi?"came out "*Posso aiutarmi?*" Instead of asking him to help me, I had asked him if I could help myself. I realized a few seconds later and tried to correct myself, but he answered me in English, saying he knew what I meant, and he would be glad to help. He unloaded two of suitcases and wished me good luck.

But then I had to transfer to a train to Padova.

This turned out to be no easy task, as I had to carry my suitcases down a staircase to the *sottopassaggio* under the train tracks, then up again to the station, where I looked at the big board to find out which track to take to Padova. Then it was back down into the tunnel and then up to the tracks again—all this in the hottest month of the summer. Not to mention that I always had to temporarily abandon two suitcases while I carried the others, continually thinking of what had happened to the Floridians just a few hours before. Italy is certainly not designed for the handicapped or elderly— or people with too many suitcases.

I arrived in Padova sweaty, smelly and low on energy, and there I committed a couple of mindless blunders that rendered me not just dripping with perspiration but positively bathed. After carrying my four suitcases, which I swear had doubled in weight, down the stairs to the *sottopassaggio*, I pushed and pulled my luggage along until I spied, praise God, an elevator to take me back up, presumably right into the station. But no, it took me back to the tracks; I hadn't gone far enough in the tunnel to get to the station. So back down I went, embarrassed because the people above who had been waiting for the elevator couldn't fit in with all my baggage cramming the small space.

The heat and embarrassment so flustered me that I made an even more egregious mistake a moment later. Exiting the elevator in the tunnel, I blundered down the corridor and took the next set of steps up to the station—at least I thought it was the station, but it turned out to be more stairs up to the tracks. By now I couldn't decide whether to cry or laugh, but I didn't have long to grieve, since I was also freaking out about the suitcases I had left in the tunnel. Back down one more time, and finally I made it up to the station. Once there, I sat on a bench and tried to dry off for half an hour before calling Gino to come pick me up.

Fortunately, Gino had taken care of all the negotiations for our apartment, which was on the top floor of a four-story complex. *La padrona*—the landlady—managed the rental for her son. Gino had tried to pay Signora Maggiore in cash, but she was elderly and didn't like to go out to the bank, so he set up a direct deposit into her account. Then he would take the money out of my paycheck each month. The apartment cost 1 million lira per month, about $500, plus another $200 or so for utilities and condominium fees, all of which, thankfully, Gino would take care of paying. I would reimburse him from my salary.

Because Gino had made all the arrangements, I almost missed out on meeting Signora Maggiore, which would have been unfortunate, as circumstances soon would show. But luckily she showed up just before Gino left, and he quickly introduced us. She was a slender, dignified and well dressed elderly lady who spoke no English, but my Italian was sufficient for situations such as meeting people.

"*Piacere di conscerLa,*" I said, using the polite form.

"*Piacere,*" she replied with a kind and welcoming smile.

Gino had already shown me around the apartment, so he left me to unpack. I set about plugging in the lamps that had been disconnected by the previous tenants, and in so doing, I found out that there are four different types of electrical outlets in Italy, and my apartment was represented by all four. At first I thought there were only two types, one with two holes and one with three. However, I soon discovered that the outlets came in two sizes, small prong holes and large prong holes. I also discovered that you cannot plug a lamp with two prongs into an outlet with three. I'd like to say that I only tried this because it was dark, but it really wasn't. There was a two-pronged lamp on a table next to a three-hole receptacle, so maybe that's where it had been plugged in before? Well, it worked—for a fraction of a second. But then it didn't, and neither did anything else in the apartment.

I located the circuit breakers in the laundry closet, but they hadn't been tripped. I turned them off and on several times to be sure, but still there was no electricity, and it would be very dark in another half hour. Faced with unpacked luggage in a strange apartment that was about to be plunged into total darkness, I was grateful I remembered the landlady's name.

I went downstairs to the mailboxes to determine which flat was hers and found it was on my floor. Indeed, it was right across from me. Back upstairs, I rang her bell. No answer, so I went back and made my bed. At least I would have a place to sleep tonight.

Then, *per fortuna*, I heard someone in the hall and discovered Signora Maggiore returning to her apartment.

"Signora, ho un problema. Non c'è l'elettricità."

My paltry Italian skills were paying off. She said she would go downstairs to find someone who could fix the power. Apparently this man knew where the main breakers were, because though I never saw him, the lights magically came on in about ten minutes. Signora Maggiore returned, and we had a conversation full of pointing and gesturing about outlets, adapters and extension cords. She gave me some adapters and cords, although later I discovered some in a closet and returned the ones she had given me.

In the next few days, I visited two bicycle shops and a second-hand store, and I felt good that I had been able to communicate necessary information in Italian. The owner of one shop even complimented me for learning so much in just a few days, though I didn't tell him that I had been studying on my own off and on for several years. If I had started to feel a bit smug about my ability to communicate with the locals, that confidence soon vanished when I had to deal with a non-functioning gas water heater. Signora Maggiore came on Saturday with Agnese, a cleaning lady, to put up the curtains and wax the floor. She also brought me a drying rack for my clothes. It was a simple matter to tell her that "*l'acqua calda non funzione.*" She made a phone call, and amazingly, a repairman showed up in half an hour. The ensuing fifteen-minute conversation between *la signora*, the repairman and a neighbor left me completely baffled. I understood *sporco* (dirty), *pulito* (clean) and *rotto* (broken), but very little else. Because of the way the repairman was pointing at things, I surmised he was saying that he could take it out and clean it, but he might discover that it was broken and have replace it— or he could just replace the whole thing now. But if he took it out, the stove would have to be shut off, because they were on the same gas line.

It couldn't have taken fifteen minutes just to say these few things, however, so I wondered what else had transpired in this lengthy back-and-forth. After a while, they discovered that the previous day I had turned on the gas to another water heater that was in the *bagno*—the bathroom—which had seemed to me a logical step. But for reasons I still don't fully understand, it was the wrong thing to do. The repairman turned it off, and suddenly the one in the kitchen worked again.

The only drawback was that the hot water for the bagno had to come all the way from the *cucina,* while the heater in the bagno sat idle. Nevertheless, I was told to leave the bathroom gas *sempre chiuso* (always closed), and I did. So I had hot water again, for about a month anyway, until the kitchen heater gave out completely and Signora Maggiore had to replace it with a new one, which, she said, "*Costa molto.*"

I had a full week before school started and my family arrived, though I had meetings and preparations to attend to at the school. I went to the train station to purchase bus tickets and was able to purchase a "carnet" of tickets for a reduced price. What kind of Italian word is that? It was a packet of thirty tickets that cost the equivalent of about $20. When boarding a bus, one inserts a ticket in a slot, and the ticket is stamped with the date and time. The ticket is then valid for one hour, even if one changes buses. I realized that I would go through a couple of carnets a month, since I would need at least two tickets per day to commute to school.

Using my Italian-English dictionary to read the signs on the wall of the station, I discovered that it was possible to purchase an *abbonamento mensile*, a monthly bus pass, for about $22.

I went back to the window, and asked the *impiegato*, "*Lei parla inglese?*"As I was soon to discover, not many government officials in Padova spoke English, and this man was no exception. Undaunted, I set my lira on the counter and announced, *"Voglio comprare un abbonamento mensile urbano."*

What followed was about a one-minute explanation in which the only words I understood were *passaporto* and *foto tessera.* The official pointed to some forms over to the side, and I took one home to read. After doing my best to translate the form and fill in the blanks, I concluded that I had understood the most important parts of the instructions already, although as in the case of the hot water repairman, I wondered why it took so many words to say, "Fill out the form, get your picture taken in the little booth over there and come back with your passport and money."

However, I assumed that I would soon have a monthly pass, and I realized that in the meantime, I was wasting money by using my carnet of tickets. My family could use these tickets when they arrived, but the next two days I had to work late at school and the ticket office was closed after I left work, so I had to keep using my tickets.

One morning the bus was so crowded that I couldn't reach the ticket validating machine. I was happy to have saved myself from using up another ticket, and I didn't feel bad because it wasn't my fault. But it started me thinking. I noticed that a few other people didn't always use the validating machine, and in the week I had been in Padova, I had never seen a bus driver check anyone's ticket. Why, in a country of people notorious for side-stepping the law, did most of the people always board buses with tickets in hand, even though there seemed to be no penalty for not having a ticket or not validating it if you had one?

The next day, I left work in plenty of time to get my *abbonamento*. I had run out of tickets, but I wasn't concerned because I was on my way to obtaining a monthly pass, which in a way would make this bus trip legal, even if only retroactively. However, halfway to the station, I found out why people use tickets—the bus police! Two uniformed men boarded the bus and announced something in Italian. Soon everyone except me was lined up to show validated tickets. I sat, agonizing about what to do, as my face turned deeper and deeper red. How could I explain that I was on my way to buy a monthly pass at that very moment? As the police reached the end of the line, I was now not only red but starting to sweat. What to do? I stood and showed my day-old ticket.

"*Deve scendere*," one officer said, pointing to the date on my ticket.

"*Non parlo italiano*," I answered, although I quickly realized that I had recognized the words, "You must get off."

The officer turned away and joined his partner, who was arguing with a woman who had not validated her ticket. I stood in my spot, wondering what would come next. The woman was saying she had put her ticket in the machine, but it didn't print. Then the official took her ticket, inserted it in the machine and showed her that it worked flawlessly. They engaged in a few more words with her and then exited the bus with me still standing there waiting for my punishment. I had escaped eviction and the price of a ticket, but at a high price in lost dignity and embarrassment. It took another two minutes for my face to stop burning.

I later learned that one of the British teachers' aides who worked at my school went the whole year without buying a bus ticket. She said the police had boarded her buses seven times during the year, but she always played dumb and spoke only English, and they always let her get by.

When I reached the station, I happily purchased my *abbonamento mensile*. I had filled out the forms correctly enough to satisfy the clerk and had my photo and passport in hand. Clutching my pass, I celebrated by hopping on the first bus I saw outside the station. I had no place in particular where I had to be, nor did I really know much about the city, so wherever the bus took me would be an adventure.

I rode for a while and then got off and walked around. I found a fruit store that had peaches for sale for 5,000 lira, about $2.50. Was that for one peach or a carton? I didn't want to display my ignorance, so I asked, "*Quanto costano dieci pesche*?" The signora put ten on her scale and gave me a price, which made me understand that the price was per kilogram. The total was reasonable, and as my family would be arriving next day, I bought all ten.

I also found a bike shop that had two nice used bicycles at a decent price, although I had no idea at the time what constituted a good deal, since the other shops I had visited had none for sale. I didn't want to buy the first bikes I saw and then find out they were cheaper elsewhere, so I declined and took the bus back home.

Lucy and the girls were in Rome and would arrive in Padova the next day. I had been in town for nine days and had settled in fairly well. I knew where the grocery stores in my neighborhood were and could negotiate the city by bus. Our apartment was simple but adequate, and I was settling in well at school. Making it on my own had been relatively easy, but now I had two unwilling and unhappy teens on the way, fighting the heat, jet lag, mountains of luggage and possibly a tired and cranky mom.

Chapter 7: Reunited in a new land

When my heavily laden family arrived, we had a happy reunion. They had enjoyed a day in Rome to recover and see a few sights. Both Suzye and Lindsey wore the standard uniform for American teens of that era—tight tops that showed a couple of inches of their bellies and low-riding jeans. Suzye had shocking pink hair. Well, they were going to stand out in the crowd here, but I chalked it up as something young people have to go through at some stage. Lucy and I had come of age in the 1960s, and we knew a few things about self expression through hair and clothing. I had once displayed a magazine article prominently on my bedroom door written by a liberal-thinking mother; it had been titled: *Keep out of my kids' hair!* Lucy herself had once fully embraced the age of the mini-skirt.

We all needed bus passes and bicycles, but I soon learned that used bicycles were not that easy to come by in Padova. The city was full of cyclists of all ages, and most of the bikes were old and battered, but not many were for sale. I met an American who explained that people prefer worn bikes because newer bikes were quickly stolen. If I bought new bikes, he said, I could expect to have to replace them several times during the year because of theft, especially if we parked near the train station.

I visited a bike shop near my work three or four times in the next few weeks, but the proprietor never had any used bikes. Every time, though, he would name a day when I should come back again, usually Monday but sometimes Wednesday. I was beginning to wonder if I was getting the runaround because I was a foreigner. I tried going back to the first bike shop I had visited, but the bikes I had seen had been sold, and the shop had nothing else to offer. I should have grabbed them when I had the chance. Now I was no longer so concerned about saving a few lira—I just wanted a bike. Buses were great for getting to work, but they ran infrequently on weekends and didn't always go to places I wanted to go.

I easily walked Suzye and Lindsey through the steps of buying bus passes. *"Due abbonamenti studenti, per favore,"* I said. I wondered if the girls were duly impressed by my language prowess, but they didn't say anything.

We bought a carnet for Lucy, thinking that she wouldn't be using the bus often enough to justify an abbonamento mensile, though within two weeks we realized she needed a monthly pass too.

Lucy tried on her own to get a pass, but to her chagrin, she was denied an abbonamento. She told me that out of the flurry of words the clerk used to explain the refusal, she recognized the familiar phrase *"permesso di soggiorno."* These words mean "permission to stay," and it was a phrase that would both tease and haunt us during our entire time in Italy. Why I had been able to buy passes before with only a passport and Lucy could not was, like many things in Italy, inexplicable. Maybe because she was not able to speak much Italian yet, or maybe because she was a blonde and looked more German than Italian. Perhaps the clerk who had given my pass should have asked to see my permesso di soggiorno and either didn't remember or didn't care.

In any event, Lucy was frustrated nearly to tears, both with being turned down and her lack of ability to understand Italian. I decided we should try again, with me doing the talking, but also making sure not to see the same clerk. I tried to act relaxed and confident so as not to arouse suspicion about my foreignness. *"Un abbonamento mensile per mia moglie,"* I said, handing over her photo, passport and application form. The clerk stared at Lucy's passport for a few moments, but then he closed it and issued her pass. We had bypassed the need for a permesso di soggiorno, although that wouldn't be the last time we were asked for that elusive document.

Lucy never again had a problem with her bus pass, though. She was able to renew it each month without question, as the officials never examine a person's paperwork upon renewal. In fact, the renewal process could be handled without words, because at the end of each month, one just had to put the appropriate amount of lira on the counter with the expired bus pass, and the officials automatically renewed the pass.

Lucy and the girls had arrived in Padova on September 9, 2001. Two days later, I was in school in the computer lab when one of the other teachers told me, "It looks like an airplane has run into the World Trade Center in New York." My first thought was that a small private plane might have clipped a wing on the corner of one of the towers. I didn't hear anything else until I got home that evening, and then we received what I thought was a strange phone call from Silvia, who had been an exchange student in our home during the previous year. She wanted to know if our daughter Sandy, who lived in Washington DC, was all right. Why would Silvia be asking that, I wondered? Then she told me what had happened.

"Turn on the TV," I told Lucy. I thanked Silvia for calling, and our family sat down to watch the mind-numbing images that now played over and over. We didn't have to comprehend Italian to grasp the magnitude of the disaster, and we could understand the people who were being interviewed as long as the over-dubbed Italian translations weren't too loud. We saw that the Pentagon had been targeted as well, and we contacted Sandy as soon as we could. She was fine; she had been sent home from work in DC and walked to a friend's apartment, where they watched the horrible scenes on the news.

We received notice from our airline that our flight to America scheduled for September 12 had been canceled and that we could apply for a refund. It was only then that we recalled we had purchased round trip tickets because there had been a special offer, and round trip fare had been cheaper than one-way tickets. We could have asked for money back, but it seemed crass to take advantage of a shocking situation that had so crippled our country.

By being abroad, we were spared some of the shock of 9/11. We received a lot of sympathy from the people we met. It seemed that every Italian we met had distant relatives in America. That connection, combined with the recollection that the American armed forces had helped free Italians from the brutal regimes of Mussolini and Hitler only 55 years earlier, contributed to a still strong pro-American sentiment in Italy. We noticed an extra contingent of gun-toting police outside the McDonald's restaurant near the train station, as it was the most visible representation of our country in Padova, but we were otherwise insulated from most of the trauma experienced by our compatriots in America. The heightened security and focus on terrorism did affect our padrona, however. Signora Maggiori revealed to us that she had purchased a gas mask because she had *paura dei terroristi*—fear of the terrorists.

Chapter 8: Teaching for the Godfather

Adjusting from teaching high school to fifth grade took some doing. Catherine, the other fifth grade teacher, provided support and advice, as did Angela, the new elementary school director. When I saw Angela in action, I was amazed that Gino had once considered hiring me instead of her for that position. She was a born leader who had been with the school for several years and knew all the routines. I almost always arrived early at school to set up for the day, but Angela was often already there. We were both workaholics—we had that in common so we became mutual admirers and fast friends.

The school was British in its techniques and Italian in its curriculum. Since all the teachers except me were from England, I had another language barrier to overcome. The garbage can was the bin, the elevator the lift and vacations were the holidays. I was shocked when Angela asked me if I needed more rubbers for my classroom, but then she held up a box of pencil erasers. When I mentioned being overwhelmed with all the preparations for teaching a new grade level in a different school system, one of the male teachers told me, "Well, keep your pecker up." Apparently, that's Brit-speak for cheer up, or keep your head up. In American slang, a pecker is . . . well, another part of one's anatomy. I also did a double take when a teacher entered my room during our preparation week and asked if I had taken the guillotine from the workroom. Wow, what kind of discipline system did they have at this school? It reminded me of an anecdote of a misbehaving boy whose parents had put him in a private

Catholic school renowned for shaping up rule-breakers. To the parents' surprise, the boy became an ideal student on the first day. When they asked him why he had changed so suddenly, he replied, "Well, I heard this school was tough on troublemakers. Then when I saw that guy nailed up on the wall, I knew they were really serious." Anyway, I didn't have the guillotine, which I later found out is what we Yanks call a paper cutter.

Every lesson I wrote took four times longer to conduct than I expected. I had planned to start each English lesson with some free writing. In my high school classes, five minutes of free writing had usually sufficed to spark some creativity. I tried this on the first day of class in Padova, asking my pupils to write about their summer vacations.

"What do you mean by vacation?" Giulia asked.

"You know, *vacanza*, I said, accidentally violating a school rule about not speaking Italian in class.

"I think he means holidays," Anna added. Oh, those! Now everybody understood, but they kept asking for help with spelling, vocabulary and sentence structure, even after I repeatedly explained that these details were unimportant in free writing. After fifteen minutes of this torture, most of the students had written only two sentences. That was the last time I tried free writing with this class.

I had not adequately taken into account that English was not their native language. Most were Italians whose parents wanted them to grow up bilingual, but the kids didn't start learning English until they enrolled in the school. One of them had just enrolled the previous year. On the plus side, I didn't have to spend as much time planning lessons as I had expected, because a science lesson I anticipated to last an hour might stretch out into four hours, which covered two weeks of science classes.

Two days into the term, Gino asked me to see him in his office. He hemmed and hawed for a minute, and then told me that a mother had complained that her daughter couldn't understand me. "You have an American accent, and you might be speaking too quickly," he said. Probably so, I agreed. I made an effort to slow down. Two weeks later, Gino told me that the girl was doing fine.

A pleasant difference between my fifth graders and the average American high school student emerged: Every student was engaged and conscientious. I had never taught at a private school before, and these kids were a joy to teach. They did their homework. They loved history and science, and they peppered me with questions, especially when we started studying the human body.

Students of all grades are tested at the end of the year by officials from the Italian school system, and I found this to be a source of healthy student anxiety. The kids mentioned the tests often enough that I realized this was a factor in why they were so conscientious. One day Stefano raised his hand and told me that I wasn't working them hard enough to get them ready for the tests. Of course, I gave a typical teacher answer: "Don't worry, Stefano, I know exactly what I'm doing."

After class, I quickly made the rounds of the other teachers to ask them what I was doing, or supposed to be doing.

"I've never heard of any student who's failed the end-of-year test," Catherine reassured me. "We're both at the same spot in the curriculum. Don't worry. They'll be just fine." Aha! So I hadn't lied to Stefano.

Catherine explained that finals were oral exams that amounted to little more than the examiners calling each student out of class, glancing at his or her work portfolio and then asking each to give a description of what he or she had learned during the year. The kids seemed to be far more serious about the tests than the teachers were, but I guessed that the mere possibility of being the first child to fail kept my class motivated, and it contributed to my belief in the value of year-end testing.

I still wasn't sure why Gino hired me, because the school was only supposed to employ teachers certified in the British system. Only one other American worked at the school, though not as a teacher. Like me, he was paid *sotto il tavolo*. Gino had helped Maurice get a student visa—although in reality Maurice was a teachers' aide and not a student at the school. Just out of college in the spring, he had taken a summer trip to Italy and then decided to stay longer before starting the job hunt in the United States. One day a school inspector came for a scheduled appointment, and Gino informed me that Pamela would be teaching a special mathematics lesson to my class that day, while I sat in the back with Maurice as a classroom helper. That way if the inspector came to my classroom, he would find a British teacher conducting the lesson. Everyone was on high alert to do their best that day, but it turned out that the inspector assigned was an acquaintance of Gino's, and he never even stepped inside a classroom. Catherine said she found the inspector in Gino's office, sharing a bottle of wine and helping Gino fill out the forms needed for the annual re-certification.

I clearly had been offered the job because of my desire for a one-year gig. Gino usually found his teachers through a British agency that promised teachers two-year contracts. Gino also could avoid paperwork and agency fees by hiring me directly. Our contract was entirely oral and turned out to be a good deal for both parties.

I heard some gossip that he also hired me because he had experienced some problems with the previous teacher, and some parents were threatening to pull their kids out of the school. I had a strong résumé and twenty years of teaching experience, and if he hired through the British system, he would have had to take his chances with someone just out of the university. With tuition at nearly 1,000 euros a month (Italy transitioned from lira to euros during our time in the country), if three dissatisfied parents pulled their children out of the school, Gino would lose more than 25,000 euros. No wonder he was so concerned that one of my students couldn't understand me during the first week of school.

Payday was the last day of the month. I'm not sure how the British teachers were paid, but I had to go into Gino's office after school. He slid open a desk drawer full of neatly stacked bills, moved aside a loaded pistol and counted out a pile of cash. Okay, I may be exaggerating about the pistol; I couldn't actually see inside the drawer, but that's the way Maurice and I imagined it.

It's true that Gino was a sort of benign version of "The Godfather." A short, dapper man about fifty years old with dark hair, brown eyes and slightly wavy hair, he looked a bit like Al Pacino. Gino had founded the school with his wife fourteen years prior. A shrewd businessman, he underpaid his employees, but he also took care of them. He arranged housing for the new teachers and used his connections to help out in whatever ways he could. If one of his British teachers had car trouble, he would send out Bruno, one of the bus drivers, to take care of it. Our apartment originally lacked an oven and washing machine, but a few words from Gino resulted in their prompt installation, at his own expense. If Gino wanted something for the school, he had no need for budget committees or red tape. It would done without question.

With all that Gino did for his staff, I was happy to find a way to help his family as well. His son Giulio was in his final year of a private high school that had an International Baccalaureate program, and he had a huge thesis due. He had written some thirty pages on his chosen topic, the American stock market, but he was short another ten pages and had run out of things to say. I helped Giulio clean up his grammar and gave him some ideas and references for other aspects he could cover. In fact, in describing what he could write about, I probably wrote a few of his pages myself.

This favor paid off nicely later when I asked for a couple of days of unpaid leave to extend one of our school vacations. I explained my plans to Angela, and early one morning on my way to my classroom, I overheard Angela and Gino discussing my request in Angela's office. "I can't refuse him after the help he gave Giulio," Gino said. However, Angela explained to me later, because it might create hard feelings with the other teachers, Gino had instructed her to tell anyone who asked where I was that I was ill. When Gino went to pay me at the end of the month, I reminded him that I had taken some unpaid days off. He paid me the usual amount, shrugged and said not to worry about it. We were friends. I had respected him. I had done him a favor. He would take care of me. After all, he was the Godfather.

Chapter 9: Meeting, eating, Italian style

Finding a church in Italy that's not Catholic can be a challenge. Choices are very few. Though I was raised a Catholic, I had long attended a non-denominational Protestant church in Gig Harbor as an adult—as had Lucy and all the kids. We first tried Padova's Italian version of the Assemblies of God, an organization that is independent of the American denomination of the same name. The main problem we had was that our language skills weren't far enough advanced to understand much of anything that the pastor said. When the service ended, we quickly exited, and Suzye and Lindsey immediately started walking home. Lucy and I paused for a moment, unsure whether to follow the girls or go back inside.

I sensed this would be a turning point. I had led my family to Italy to meet Italians, and surely those who shared our faith would be among the most amicable. I gathered my courage and went back inside, and Lucy followed.

Someone at the church must speak English. Yes, I was told, Stefano and Nancy Mammi speak English quite well. Someone ran to find them, and not only were Stefano and Nancy extremely helpful in our search for a church but they soon become close friends.

Stefano was a chemistry professor at the university in Padova. He did post-graduate studies in the United States, where he met and married Nancy Jenkins. They moved back to Padova, Stefano's home town, when they finished their schooling. Nancy, who had adapted to the Italian language and culture, also taught at the university. They recommended that we try International Christian Fellowship, which held services in English with a translator who rendered the sermon into Italian. Coincidentally, Nancy was from Everett, Washington, just a couple of hours from where we live in Gig Harbor. They had three boys, the oldest of whom was about Lindsey's age, and they invited us to dinner at their house the following weekend.

Next Sunday, we attended ICF and met Steve and Patti Gray, the missionary couple who headed the ministry. In another strange coincidence, they were actually from Gig Harbor and knew some of the same people we knew. They had been missionaries in Italy since 1986, but they started the church in Padova just three years before our arrival. They invited us over for lunch after the service, and thus began another close long-term friendship.

The church service was longer and the worship more demonstrative than we were used to, but the congregation sang many of the familiar modern Christian songs, and for the most part we felt much more comfortable than we had at the Italian church the previous week. African immigrants comprised about half of those attending, with perhaps another quarter of the members consisting of Eastern Europeans, and the rest a mixture from all over the world. Only a few native Italians attended, which was understandable, since the church's primary mission was to the international community. Having the sermon translated sentence-by-sentence from English to Italian also provided us with valuable language lessons. We would continue to attend ICF during our entire year, and we still go back every time we visit Padova.

During the next week, Patti took Lucy on an excursion to one of the large grocery stores and gave her an invaluable cultural lesson in shopping, Italian style. Lucy returned from the trip excited at her discoveries.

The first lesson came in the parking lot. To use a shopping cart, you put a euro into a slot to free the cart. When you were done, your euro was returned; thus every cart is returned to the proper location and strays are never found in parking lots or alleys.

Once inside the stores, Lucy continued: "I was getting some dirty looks when I starting picking out produce. Patti explained that to touch fruit and vegetables, you first put on disposable plastic gloves. Then you put the produce in a plastic bag and weigh it, and you push a button on the front of the scale, which has the name and a picture of the product. At the end, the scale spits out a sticker that you fasten to the bag with a price and bar code, so the checkout clerk doesn't have to weigh or price the produce.

"And speaking of the checkout clerks, they're seated on stools instead of standing the way American cashiers must do. It seems kinder, more civilized, somehow."

Some of the products common in American cooking were either not available in Italy or existed under obscure names.

"Cottage cheese," she said. "They do have it here, but it's *fiocchi di latte*, flakes of milk. They don't have brown sugar, *zucchero marrone*, but there's something like it called *zucchero di canna*, cane sugar."

"That's great," I replied, "but it means nothing if you still can't make chocolate chip cookies."

"Sorry about that one," she said. "There's still no chocolate chips. But I did find out that baking soda and baking powder exist, sort of. They just aren't exactly the same chemical combination as the American versions, but I'd never have found them without Patti's help. The baking soda is with the bottled water, because people use it to carbonate their water."

Refried beans and bean dip, Bisquick, cheddar cheese, condensed sweetened milk, tortilla chips and graham crackers—essential ingredients in some of my favorite meals and desserts—were not found under any name. Only a few stores had peanut butter and oatmeal. The father of one of my students was an officer at a nearby U.S. military base, and his wife procured some favorite American staples for us. Lucy made a favorite family recipe, magic cookie bars, that I shared with Italian acquaintances, and one of them asked me for the recipe. I gave it to her but realized it would do her little good. Four of the key ingredients weren't available in the Italian supermarket: chocolate chips, sweetened condensed milk, sweetened coconut flakes and graham crackers.

On the other hand, the vast array of cheeses overwhelmed us. A grocery store might have 100 different types of cheese, and a *formaggeria* more than 150—although none quite like American cheddar. Provolone, we found will substitute in a pinch. At first, we didn't try any of the unfamiliar cheeses. I enjoyed free lunches all year in the school cafeteria, and if Lucy and the girls happened to be around at the time, Gino said they were welcome to dine for free as well. One or two kinds of cheeses were available daily, changing throughout the week. Out of habit, I first ignored them. Then it occurred to me that eating what is offered is part of the cultural experience, and I found I had been missing out! Each type was delicious in its own way. The cafeteria didn't have a menu, so I have no idea what types of cheeses I was eating, but I learned they are almost all excellent. Only very infrequently did we come across a stinker, so to speak.

Lucy still cooked up many of our favorite American meals, but she soon realized how easy it was to create gourmet Italian meals without going to a restaurant. Just stop at a *pastificio* (not a *pasticceria*, which sells pastries) and you could buy homemade ravioli, lasagne, gnocchi or any variety of local pasta, along with a choice of sauces. Take it home and heat it up, and you could cook (and eat) like a culinary *maestro*. Even the grocery stores had excellent fresh and dried pasta. Other specialty stores sold homemade sauces. A *macelleria*—butcher shop—sold choice cuts of beef, pork, chicken or turkey, thinly sliced for easy frying. It is fixed in their blood for Italians to buy from small farmers, so the meats and poultry was all more flavorful—not to mention more healthful because of lack of additives.

Rabbit and horse meat were also readily available, though we didn't try those. We boarded horses on our property in Gig Harbor, and we certainly couldn't have brought ourselves to eat horse meat. At least, we thought we couldn't. Yes, we could, Patti corrected me.

"You eat in the school cafeteria, don't you?" she said. I nodded. "Well, then you're eating horse meat." Steve and Patti had both worked part time at the school the previous year, and they said the cafeteria served horse regularly. "You just didn't know what it was," she explained. Great! Well, I guess we like horse meat, because all the meals served in the cafeteria were excellent.

Fruits and vegetables in Italy were fresh and uncommonly delicious. I never knew that tomatoes and celery had flavors until we started buying them from the Italian markets. We also found a shop called a *rosticceria* or *tavola calda,* sort of "fast food" that's ready to take home, but it had been prepared with traditional slow methods. At a good rosticceria, the food was restaurant quality, so one could save money and still bring home a complete meal.

And speaking of good healthy eating, I read that the average life expectancy for a male in the United States is seventy-six, while it is eighty for Italian males. For females, it's eighty-one in the States and eighty-five in Italy.

"I've come up with a plan," I told Lucy. "When I turn seventy-five, I'll move to Italy full time. That should add four more years to my life."

"Great," she said dryly. "And where do I fit in with this brilliant plan?"

"Of course, you can come with me, but if you don't want to come right away, you can always come a few years later. You'll have more time to think about it."

"It's hard to believe it could be so simple," she added. "It makes you wonder why nobody else has thought of that."

"Oh, it gets more complicated, but I've got the next step figured out too. If we get a house in Tuscany, it will only be a few minutes from San Marino, where men live to be eighty-three. Once I reach my Italian age limit, it won't be too tough to just move across the border."

"Sounds foolproof," she said. "You should have been a scientist instead of a teacher."

"There is a downside," I admitted. "Women in San Marino only live to be eighty-four, so you're going to have to stay behind in Tuscany to get your extra year."

"Well, I'm almost a year older than you," she said. "So if we both more to San Marino, we'll die at the same time. Maybe we can find a buy-one-get-one-free burial service and save our kids some money."

Chapter 10: Adjustment agonies

Meanwhile, Suzye and Lindsey made it clear to us that they hated living in Italy. "I'm miserable all the time," Lindsey said. "Why can't I go home and live with one of my friends?"

This was a tough question. I didn't want to say that we didn't trust her, but it was partly true. Saying that would make staying in Italy her punishment, which would only add to her frustration and anger.

"You need to grow up, get out of your shell, get some gumption and learn to adapt to new places and situations," I wanted to say, but I held my tongue because it sounded too abrupt. Instead, we gently tried to encourage her to make friends with people her age at the church. She resisted, and the vibes she gave off—the way she dressed and her cool indifference—didn't exactly attract people to her.

Suzye was not as vocal, but she moped and cried, and we knew she felt the same way. In a struggle to find her identity, she changed her hair color numerous times. After two weeks of pink, we were glad when she dyed it brown, but in another two weeks, she changed it to black. A month later, she tried to turn it to blond, with only moderate success, as it came out orange instead. A week later she tried blond again and had better luck.

Missing their friends seemed to be the biggest complaint, and they would never meet anyone new the way things were going. They took the city bus to my school to take their online classes and had almost no opportunities to meet people their own ages. Lucy and the girls started taking Italian classes at Inlingua language institute, but the school only offered private lessons, so they still had no chance to make friends. The classes were also so expensive that they threatened to shatter our budget in the first month of our stay.

Lucy found group classes at the Bertrand Russell Language School, an improvement because the classes were less costly and allowed Lucy, Suzye and Lindsey the opportunity to meet people, even if they weren't Italians.

Previously the girls had not been interested in attending an Italian high school, but after a few lonely weeks, they changed their minds. Lucy investigated the possibilities. Officials at the first school said Suzye and Lindsey couldn't attend without a permesso di soggiorno, but another school said their enrollment would be no problem. We were gradually learning a lesson about Italian bureaucracy: If one official says something can't be done, don't give up right away. Just ask a completely different official. By October 4, the girls were on their way to their first classes at Instituto Gramsci, a twenty-minute bus ride and only a fifteen-minute walk from my school. On their first day, they met some friendly students who spoke some English, and within a few days, some girls had invited them out to a dance club, the first of many such invitations that were to come. By the end of October, they had done a turn-about. They still had moments of homesickness, they said, but now they wanted to stay in Italy for the year. Well, that's what they would say one day, but the next they might be begging us to allow them go home again.

One thing that required a difficult adjustment on the part of their parents was the Italian custom of events occurring at incredibly late hours, by American standards. The dance clubs didn't usually open until around 11 p.m., and even then many people didn't arrive until midnight. We never would have let the girls stay out until 2 a.m. or later in America, but now we faced a conflict. We wanted the girls to be in school, to have friends and go out with them. If we said no to the late hours, we would essentially be dooming Suzye and Lindsey to a friendless year. We wanted to meet their friends, which we did. The friends were good students and seemed very normal and nice; they told us the late hours were just the way it was in Italy and that our girls would be safe with them. After a lot of questions and discussions, we agreed to let the girls stay out late. The first few times, we were waiting up when they came home.

At 2:30 a.m., Lucy was reading a book and I was dozing on the couch, my book having dropped to the floor. Lucy roused me when she heard the girls putting the key in the door and entering the living room.

"Safe and sound, I see," Lucy said. "How did it go?"

"We had a great time," Suzye answered. "We met a lot of nice people at the dance club. It was really fun."

"You don't have to worry about us going out with Erica and her friends," Lindsey assured us. "We felt very safe. Erica was a little disappointed to have to leave so early, but she was cool about it."

And so, we came to accept the girls going out at night, even though the hours did grow later. Were these late nights always so safe? Maybe not, but we never heard otherwise from Suzye and Lindsey, so our worrying gradually decreased.

The later hours applied to dinners and other forms of entertainment in Italy as well. A few of us guys from the school decided to spend an evening at a place advertising that it had "American Bowling." We arrived at around 10:30 p.m. and found the lanes empty. It didn't look like American bowling in Italy was catching on. This place isn't going to survive long, we thought.

We checked out our shoes, picked out our balls and bowled a couple of games. When we left, around midnight, I realized that every lane was in use. The bar was packed, the video game room was crowded. It's just that we had arrived so . . . early.

When people in Italy went out for dinner, it was usually around 9 p.m. We gradually adjusted, eating dinners later and later, though we didn't usually eat past 8 p.m., which might be opening time in Italy for a restaurant. In America, we sometimes went to a popular Italian restaurant in Tacoma. Once we arrived at about 7:50 p.m., only to be told they were closing for the night in a few minutes. And they called themselves an Italian restaurant!

I also had difficulty remembering when stores would be open or closed. I took a twenty-minute walk to the train station one day to check on the possibility of renting a car for a weekend trip. I strolled up to the Avis office at about 1 p.m. It was closed for their lunch break from 1 to 3 p.m. So were the Hertz and Maggiore offices. I had eaten at noon—*like normal people do, I fumed*—so now what? I walked back home, a wasted hour.

I should have consulted with Lucy, who had more shopping responsibilities and kept better track of the hours.

Most stores and offices closed around 1 p.m. or a little later so the owners and employees could go home, take a break and eat with their families. They reopened around 4 p.m. and stayed open until 7 or 8 p.m.

On another day, I fouled up in a similar way. A restaurant where I wanted to dine looked crowded at 2 p.m., so I went off to run some errands, thinking I could beat the crowds by waiting another hour to eat. Bad idea. The restaurant was closed by then. No problem, I thought, I'll just find another one. The next one was also closed, and the next and the next. I walked home on an empty stomach, hungrier but wiser.

Chapter 11: Chasing the permesso di soggiorno

With the girls happier and attending school regularly, Lucy also settled in to a more regular routine. She made friends from Japan, Israel, China and Belgium at the language school. I was the only one not studying Italian now, and the rest of my family began to catch up with me in linguistic abilities. Some other teachers at my school told me about free language classes offered by the *comune* of Padova to help *stranieri* like me fit in. After school, I headed to the office where I had been told I could find out about the free classes. This being Italy, though, no one in the office actually spoke English, but I was given a form to fill out. Then I was asked to show my passaporto and permesso di soggiorno. *"Non ho il permesso di soggiorno,"* I said. Well, come back when you have one, I was told, because you can't enroll without it.

We had danced around the requirement for this magical document when obtaining our bus passes and enrolling the girls in school, but now I would need one if I wanted to take free language classes. Travel books and websites advised that anyone staying in Italy for more than ninety days must first have a visa and then apply for a *permesso di soggiorno* within eight days from arrival. However, the advisers went on to explain that this law was not enforced and that travelers needn't go to the trouble, and they rarely did. We had decided to skip this requirement, since our housing was arranged for us by Gino. We figured that as long as we didn't break any laws, we would never be asked to show any documents other than our passports. However, having a permesso would save money on language classes and make us more legal during our stay, so we decided we would go to the Questura to get one.

The Questura is the provincial administrative headquarters of the state police. One might think that because foreigners have to register at the Questura, the agency would hire some officers who also speak English, Arab or some of the other common languages of the Mediterranean region, but that was not the case in Padova. The officers we met were mostly middle-aged men who spoke Italian exclusively. Maybe they figured that in the eight days we foreigners were here legally, we should have learned to speak Italian.

Since I had to work during the day, Lucy went to the Questura alone the next morning. She encountered large clusters of Africans and Eastern Europeans milling about in the alley alongside the Questura entrance. Her knowledge of Italian was still minimal, but she found a helpful student from Croatia who explained that she must sign up on a list posted on a plain sheet of paper taped to the fence beside the entrance gate. She signed the paper, but of course she was low on the list, since everybody waiting had already signed up. Some of them must have come long before the office opened to get their names high on the list. Almost four hours later, she finally made it inside the gate, but it was almost closing time; the office was only open three mornings a week. She was given a form and told to fill it out and bring it back in two days, along with four head shots of everyone in our family living here.

When she told me of her efforts, we were frustrated with the waste of time just to get a form, and I wished I could have been there to help. I wondered when the sign-up list was posted, so the next evening I stayed up until midnight and rode my bike to the Questura. Sure enough, there was a list posted, and it already had two names on it. I put Lucy down as number three and rode home in the dark and chill, pleased that I had been able to contribute to our efforts. We had all had our photos taken, so perhaps things would go more smoothly the next time.

Lucy arrived a few minutes before 8 a.m. the following morning, only to behold that the old list was missing and a new one had been posted. Since the list was posted on plain paper, someone in the early morning had torn down the previous night's list and made a new one. Either that, or the list I signed was not the official list, and the Questura officers replaced it when they came to work in the morning. Lucy could have signed up at the bottom of the new list, but she didn't have another four hours to waste, so she went home.

Next week, she tried again, going well before opening hours to put her name on the list and hang around. She made it inside after a two-hour wait, and an official looked over our forms. He shuffled them around for a minute and told her she needed something called a *marca da bollo*. "A what?" she asked. "*Che cosa?*" He explained again, more slowly, that she must go to a tabaccaio and get a marca da bollo. Lucy walked away, confused, and found someone in the crowd who spoke English. A helpful stranger explained that a marca da bollo is a government tax stamp that must be affixed; it is the way the fee for the document tax is paid, and she needed to go to a tobacco shop to buy one. So Lucy left the Questura and paid what amounted to around $10 for each of us, but then she would have to go back to the Questura another day.

The next time, thinking that we had everything we needed, Lucy and I returned together along with Suzye and Lindsey. Could the fourth time be charmed? No, not a chance. Our forms and marca da bollo were fine, said the smartly dressed, slightly balding middle-aged officer, but he added: *"È inoltre necessario prova di assicurazione sanitaria."*

"Cosa?" I said. *"Che cosa è assa . . . assicura. . .* whatever you said?"

"Assicurazione," he repeated. "Insurance."

We needed proof of assicurazione sanitaria, health insurance. Assicurazione is a difficult word for foreigners to pronounce, but I thought it wouldn't be difficult to provide, as Gino had taken out a traveler's insurance policy for our family to provide emergency health care coverage during the school year. I had the documents at home, and Lucy could bring them back the next time the Questura was open. *Va bene*, the man said, now that our family had come, we just needed one person to bring back the insurance and he could process our permesso.

So two days later, Lucy went for the fifth time. Unfortunately, we didn't understand that the assicurazione, of course, must be translated into Italian, and she sadly gave me this news at dinner.

I found that we were not alone in our frustration. At school I met Matthew Crestani, the father of Ryan, one of my fifth-grade students. Matthew was from Texas and had been transferred by his company to oversee its Italian operations in

Padova. His family had come in the summer, and he still had not been able to obtain a permesso, even though his company had hired an Italian who supposedly had expertise in such matters. We swapped tales of our frustration during a parent-teacher conference and shook our heads.

I was not ready to give up, but I also was not willing to spend money hiring a translator or other paid expert, so I used my limited Italian skills and a computer translation program to do my own translation. I had been meeting with an Italian teacher at my school for private lessons, and the entire next lesson was spent with her correcting my insurance papers translation. Several weeks later, translation in hand, Lucy and I returned. What other obstacles could they possibly throw in our path now? We were confident we would get our permesso, though it was now late November. We had been working on this for two months, and we were determined to see it through. We had already spent a lot of money on language schools and stood to spend much more. I wanted those free language lessons!

I saw the same man I had spoken to the last time I came, and he looked over the translation very carefully. I was confident because I knew it had been expertly translated by a native italiana, a teacher no less. But no, there was something here, he said, that didn't seem right to him. He pointed to a line that said not every illness is covered, referring to a clause about pre-existing conditions. I had wondered if that might be a problem when I translated it.

"Maybe I should leave this line of the translation out," I had suggested to Lucy. "If we want to live in Italy, we need to learn how to bypass some of the regulations. This seems like an Italian solution."

"No, that would be dishonest," she said, without hesitation. "It might be Italian, but it's not us. If we can't do this honestly, I don't want to do it."

"My thoughts exactly," I said. Actually, I was more like fifty-fifty on the idea, but Lucy's 100 percent assurance swayed me to the straight and narrow.

"Odds are, this guy is too busy to read every word anyway," I said. "He'll just glance at it to see that it's translated correctly and break out his stamp of approval. Why should he care about the details?"

But as luck would have it, he did read the fine print, and he did care. He pointed to the exact line I had worried about and indicated that my insurance was inadequate.

"But my assicurazione cover anything that happens to us in Italy," I did my best to say, "and we have no current medical problems."

He pointed to the line again, said some things I didn't completely understand, and refused to continue.

"Is there anything I can do to get my permesso," I asked?

I can take my insurance forms to the Questura in Milano, he suggested, where there is someone who reads English, and he can determine if my insurance is adequate.

Otherwise, no, there is nothing more that can be done here.

I left frustrated and a bit stunned. We had made six trips to the Questura, seven if you counted my futile midnight list-signing. If there had been another Questura in Padova, I could have tried my luck there, but there was only one, and there was no way to bypass this stubborn *impiegato*. I wondered how Lucy would feel about trying another Italian solution, *la bustarella*—the bribe—but I already knew the answer, so I walked away. The only thing I gained was insight into Italian bureaucracy. Well, there was one other thing: After many weeks of practice, I could finally pronounce assicurazione a native.

Suzye and Lindsey were enrolled in their Italian school by this time, and Lucy had already prepaid for another month of classes at Bertrand Russell, so it was time to concede defeat. We lived out our remaining months as "tourists," but more accurately, we were illegal aliens, without papers.

The acronym for "without papers" was once thought to be the origin of the unflattering word *wop*. A hundred years ago, Italians who went to America also had trouble obtaining their paperwork, but they could be hired as day laborers, paid in cash at the end of the day to avoid the need for contracts. This is also supposedly where the nickname *dago* from, as in going to work for the day. Both of these theories have since been debunked. Current wisdom is that *wop* derives from the slang word *guappo*, used mostly in the region of Campania to describe certain people as swaggerers, dandies or ruffians. Non-Italians heard Italian immigrants using it and thought it applied to all Italians. Dago, it is now believed, came from a corruption of the name Diego, once a generic derogatory term to describe anyone of Latin descent. Whatever—I still like the romanticism of the old explanations. And it added to the irony of my situation—an American *wop* to Italy and working for cash like a *dago*.

Meanwhile, I found that the Crestanis had shed their *without papers* status and finally obtained their documents, not through the hired expert but in the most Italian of ways. It seemed that son Ryan was quite a good soccer player, and he had been practicing with a team of local *ragazzi,* but with the first game only a few days away, the coach realized that Ryan couldn't play without his permesso. Not a problem, the coach said, because he had a friend at the Questura. Between the coach and the friend, the Crestani family had its paperwork in hand in plenty of time for Ryan's game. *Magari!* If only I was a soccer player!

Chapter 12: Finding our way

One thing that I think parents really loved about Italian public schools was that students attended on Saturday. The first Saturday the girls were in school, Lucy and I waltzed to the train station, picked out a random destination some ninety minutes away and bought a round-trip ticket. Our destination was the hill town of Feltre, population 20,000. It was cold, but we enjoyed wandering around with no immediate responsibilities. We found an outdoor ice arena and went skating and found a little restaurant for *pranzo*. This successful little jaunt inspired us to plan something more elaborate.

We had a four-day weekend for All Saints Day, a much more important holiday for Italians than Halloween is to Americans. We decided to head off to Assisi, Perugia and other destinations in Umbria in a rented Fiat Punto.

Drive into any city in America, and you will see uniformity. There will be the same restaurants, the same motels, the same grocery stores, hardware stores and drug stores. There will be broad roads with left turn lanes and wide sidewalks, with predictable stoplights and crosswalks. Each city looks much the same as the one before and after. While it is comforting to know that you can expect the same food at the Olive Garden in Florida as the one in Washington, what you gain from familiarity you also lose in the overall experience. Italian cities may have some features in common, but the cities were built gradually, over a span of hundreds or even thousands of years, with little input from city planners. Houses were built of stone and then added onto with bricks or a completely different type of stone. A stone archway might span a narrow stone street, connecting one house to another across the way. Narrow alleyways wound around darkly and ended at a broad piazza with a statue in the center. It was rare indeed to find a city designed with any semblance of a grid. The streets more likely followed the contours of the landscape, but in most places, there seemed to be neither rhyme nor reason for the pattern they followed.

Driving a car in Italy was both liberating and frustrating. The *autostrade* were fast, and it was easy to find our way. However, not losing our way in the country roads—that was a constant challenge. Road signs existed in just the right numbers to tease you into thinking you could find your way without intervention from a human or mechanical guide. Then, just when you started feeling confident, you reached an intersection where someone forgot to put directional signs. Or maybe the opposite, you were greeted with ten directional signs, but you were going 90 kilometers per hour and could only read five of them. Or even worse, there were nine directional signs, but none for the city you were seeking, so you had to pull out a map and find another city near your destination.

Our first destination was a small town, Caprese Michaelangelo. We knew there would be no directional signs until we were within at least 30 kilometers of arrival, so we had to keep consulting the map for larger cities that were on the way. Lucy served as navigator while Suzye and Lindsey read books and dozed in the back seat, oblivious to our directional dilemmas.

"Another round-about ahead," I warned. "Get ready to tell me which exit."

"The cities in our direction are Faenza and Forli," she said. "Watch for those."

"Got it. But wait, there are three exits, and the ones for Faenza and Forli are different."

"Oh, maybe we already passed Faenza."

"No, I would have noticed if we'd gone through it."

"I didn't say we were going through it, just near it."

And so, I circled, circled, circled until Lucy confirmed that Forli would be the best exit.

It is also not uncommon to find a sign pointing to the road you were seeking, but with no advance warning, so you had no time to slow down and turn.

"Look, that's the turnoff for San Vittore," Lucy shouted. "You just missed it. You should have gone right."

"Well, why didn't you tell me before I got there?"

"You're going too fast! I would have told you if you had slowed down when you saw an intersection."

"No problem. Here's another right turn. I'll take a right here and take another right, and the road is bound to join the route to San Vittore."

That sounded like a good plan, and it might have been—in another country. But in Italy, do not try this, ever! No country road in Italy ever goes straight or parallel to another for more than a half kilometer. Grid systems in Italy are more scarce than Etruscan ruins. A road going north gradually, imperceptibly turned to a road going west or east, and soon you'd be far off course. Take it from someone who's been there—or where ever it was we were now going instead of to San Vittore.

I was informed by an Italian I had met in Padova that Italians really have no equivalent word for a city block when giving directions. As strange as this may sound, upon reflection, I can see why this is so. Because medieval cities were usually surrounded by round or oval protective walls, their street patterns were now shaped more like spider webs, with large round piazzas in the center and the main streets fanning out from the middle in ever-increasing circles. Of course, more than a few bugs have struck the web of most cities, completely destroying any sense of symmetry. In some places, the spider probably sucked on a fermented grape and went completely berserk.

Another problem we encountered was that Italy doesn't use a straight up arrow to show you should stay on the same road. Instead the arrow points to the left, to indicate that *this road*, the one you are on, is the correct road.

"We should be taking a left in a few kilometers," Lucy said. "Watch for signs for Caprese Michelangelo or Ponte Singerna."

"Here's a sign that says Caprese Michelangelo," I said. "And it's pointing left."

"No, remember that means the road we're on is the road to Caprese," Lucy warned.

"But there really is a little road heading off to the left. What if we're supposed to take that?"

"It's too small. That can't be the way."

"When are we going to get there," Lindsey interrupted. "I have to pee. We've been driving a long time."

"Well, if you'd help us find the way instead of sleeping, maybe we'd be there now," I replied peevishly.

The solution is to use GPS, of course, but this was expensive and not so widely available in 2001. Besides, we had always been able to navigate with signs and maps, so why should this be any different? Our solution was to stop and ask for directions often, and we noticed males in Italy don't have the same reluctance to ask for directions that males in America do, a difference probably related to necessity. In fact, it was not unusual for cars in Padova to slow down and ask *me* for directions when I was on foot. I always had a ready answer: "*Mi dispiace. Sono straniero.*" Sorry, I'm a foreigner.

After some wrong turns and uncertainty (Lucy was correct; the left arrow had meant stay on the main road), we found Caprese Michelangelo, the birthplace of the famed artist. Lucy and I had recently read the Michelangelo biography *The Agony and the Ecstasy,* and knowing the details of his life heightened the significance of the experience. Suzye and Lindsey were both in the process of reading it. Suzye, in fact, was engrossed in the last fifty pages of the book and didn't want to put it down. In the logic that can only be understood by a sixteen-year-old mind, Suzye stayed in the car to finish the book and missed seeing the Buonarroti estate where Michelangelo grew up. She now regrets this, especially since it has become such an often-told family tale. Anytime anyone mentions Michelangelo or the trip to Perugia, someone—usually me—says, "Remember when Suzye stayed in the car reading Michelangelo's biography instead of going into his home?"

Another memorable family incident occurred that same day when we went to a restaurant that had been recommended to us by Steve and Patti. Fall is the time for the *funghi,* and on the drive up the remote hillside to eat, we saw dozens of cars parked by the roadside while their owners ventured into the woods to hunt the many varieties of *funghi selvataci*—wild mushroom. We found that the restaurant had an all-you-can-eat buffet, and we were fortunate to be offered the very last table.

I lost track of how many offerings were brought to our table, but it was at least fifteen when I stopped counting. Meat choices included the usual prosciutto but also much more exotic and extravagant choices such as wild boar, duck, rabbit and pigeon. But what we remember the most was the incredible variety of mushroom dishes. It reminded me of Forrest Gump's friend Bubba and his shrimp dishes—we had fried mushroom, boiled mushrooms, baked mushrooms, stuffed mushrooms, mushroom pâté, mushroom on crostini, mushroom steak, roasted mushroom, breaded mushroom, sautéed mushroom and braised mushroom. We were not used to eating mushrooms that actually had taste, but I quickly grew to appreciate the stronger-than-usual flavor, and Lucy held her own. Other than the bread and dessert, the meal was a waste of money for Suzye and Lindsey, who hadn't yet acquired the more refined appetites that they would develop only a few years later. One course was described as *tartufo,* and Lucy, not knowing the English word for *tartufo* was truffles, told the girls that these weren't mushrooms, so they ate them. I knew they were mushrooms, but I kept my mouth shut.

Suzye and Lindsey both have since developed into expert chefs and foodies who now love mushrooms, and they groan whenever I mention this dinner, because they can't believe they passed up all these gourmet offerings.

When it comes to taking life for granted during one's teenage years, though, I have to plead guilty as one of the world's worst offenders, so I tried not to judge my daughters too harshly. In fact, I never touched mushrooms until my senior year in college, when a group of friends ordered a mushroom pizza, and I had no choice—and found that I loved mushrooms. I also had little interest in family history until well into my middle years, and now I kick myself often for the questions I left unasked or the family stories I remember only vaguely. I didn't want to tell my daughters the truth, that I had done dumber things than they had and had also been a silent, self-absorbed teenager.

We lost our way several more times on the way to Assisi, and our rooms in the hostel were almost given away because we arrived two hours later than planned. We had stopped at a bar to get directions, and I had gone inside while the others waited in the car for what they thought would be two or three minutes. However, when the old men at the bar found out I was an American, they wouldn't let me leave. One of them insisted on buying me a beer and then proceeded to tell me about his experiences in the war, how he had met British General Montgomery and how he had helped the Americans and British free the country from Nazi Germany. He actually said a lot more than that, but I could only understand a tenth of it, having been living in Italy for only two months. It was a tantalizing experience, because I wanted nothing more than to be able to sit and shoot the breeze with a group of war veterans from Italy-but now that I had my wish, I couldn't capitalize on it. *Accidenti*!

After about ten minutes, Lucy and the girls came looking for me, and they got to hear another five minutes of war adventures before the friendly story-teller got in his car and led us to the hostel. We thanked him profusely, and I nodded along to another five minutes of incomprehensible stories while Lucy and the girls checked in.

Assisi is an extraordinary city virtually untouched by modern architecture. Its soft pink medieval buildings shimmer against the green backdrop of Mount Subasio.

A ruined castle—Rocca Maggiore—an imposing fortress rebuilt in the fourteenth century over an earlier fortification dating back to the time of Charlemagne, looms over the city. The spectacular complex of the Basilica of Saint Francis of Assisi, recognizable by the massive arched buttresses of the convent, is located on the western side. Saint Francis was born here in 1182, and two years after his death in 1228, construction began. Upon completion, the basilica's walls were frescoed by the best known artists of the time, including Giotto, Cimabue, Simone Martini and Pietro Lorenzetti.

It is crazy how much time and energy Italians have spent making intricate and beautiful buildings, mostly churches, but also castles, bridges, aqueducts and theaters. One would think the *italophile* that I am, I must be an art connoisseur, but it is not so. You can't walk down a street in any city center for very long without finding something mind-blowing. A work of art that gets little attention in a small city here would be a big deal if it were in the middle of Gig Harbor. Art and architecture are so commonplace that one gets accustomed to seeing them all the time, but if I stop for just a minute, I am still amazed.

It's actually not the art that impresses me the most, and it is not even the architecture. Perhaps if I had any skills as an artist or architect, I would be more affected by the subtle variations in techniques, the use of chiaroscuro and perspective, but what actually astounds me the most is the thought of how these buildings were made. While other people go inside a church to admire the frescoes and mosaics, I often find myself standing outside studying the stone work. Each slab of marble or other stone has been cut into a smooth rectangular shape by a craftsman who had no power saw with diamond tipped blades, no gas engines or electricity. I imagine myself using hand tools and trying to take a stone and form a perfect 12" x 12" x 24" block, with each side perfectly flat and smooth, and all angles a perfect ninety degrees. It seems like that in itself would be a lifetime's work, but then I try to imagine making thousands of identical blocks. Some of them had to be rounded for archways, and the rounded portions had to be perfectly symmetrical.

Then in my mind I become the builder, carrying these stones up five, six, seven stories high and aligning them perfectly. I am not standing on metal scaffolding, though. It must be made of wooden poles. There are numerous other details that continue to boggle my weak mind: the pillars and arches inside that are needed to hold up the walls and ceiling (and of course they have to be aesthetically pleasing as well as structurally sound). Decisions had to be made about what materials to use for the ceiling and roof, how to form the windows and doors, and so on. Yes, I am more of a construction worker than an artist, but Italy has beauty to offer every type of artisan.

Chapter 13: Making friends

Back home after our four-day adventure, we had better luck understanding our *padrona*, Signora Maggiore, than I had had in the bar in Assisi. She didn't care for Gino, who had negotiated our lease and refused to renegotiate when she changed her mind and wanted to raise the rate. But Gino told us they had already reached an agreement and she couldn't change the rent just before we moved in. Besides, he held the upper hand, he explained, because she was supposed to have approval from the *comune* to rent an apartment—which would mean paying more taxes—and she had bypassed that step. She regarded us as innocents abroad, though, and her animosity for Gino didn't carry over to us.

We had Signora Maggiore and her grown daughter Cristina over for dinner in November, and they returned the favor in December. We did okay communicating with basic phrases and some sign language. Signor Maggiore had died some years previously, and his wife and Cristina, a sweet-natured person with a mild developmental disability, lived alone. The apartment we were renting belonged to her son Massimo and his wife, but they were in Mexico working on a horse ranch. Signora Maggiore spoke clearly and used standard Italian instead of dialect, so we were always encouraged after we talked to her.

The teachers at high school, though, were not happy with the progress and attitudes of Suzye and Lindsey. We had a talk with the principal, and he said the teachers didn't understand why the girls weren't trying harder at their classwork the way the other foreign students were. The school had made an effort to put our girls in the best classes, but they weren't doing their homework or participating in class discussions. As our conversation continued, I realized that we were at cross purposes. The other foreign students were immigrants who came to Italy for a good education and a better life, so they were highly motivated. Suzye and Lindsey simply wanted to go to school to make friends and experience Italian culture. They were keeping up with their American school requirements in their free time, and they would probably not get credit for their work in the Italian school, so they saw little reason to worry about it.

We explained the principal's concerns to Suzye and Lindsey.

"Dad, we have no hope of understanding the teachers" Lindsey said. "They talk the entire time, and I'd be better off working on my Italian language workbooks in class. But I tried this, and they said it was 'rude' when I did that."

"The history teacher is crazy," Suzye said. "I put my backpack on the floor and knelt down beside it to get my stuff out, and he went berserk! He grabbed me and pulled me to my feet and started yelling at me—spit flying out of his mouth—telling me how disrespectful I was for sitting on the floor. I thought he was going to hit me. The other kids gathered around me and told him to stop, and then they told me to just ignore him, that he was an unbalanced, senile old man. They said it was no use to try to change anything because teachers in Italy can't be fired."

However, Suzye and Lindsey understood the merits of the principal's point of view. We agreed that Lindsey would withdraw from Gramsci at Christmas break and start taking Italian classes with Lucy at Bertrand Russell. Suzye opted to stay in Gramsci and work harder. Part of the issue still had to do with friends. Lindsey was in classes with students her own age who didn't speak much English. She had been bored, lost and largely friendless at school. Suzye was in classes with senior students, and since Italians attend public schools for 13 years, the students were 18 and 19 years old and spoke English reasonably well. Outside of school, Lindsey ended up joining Suzye and her older friends for social activities. Suzye agreed it was hard to listen all day to teachers who lectured during every class, but she would put up with boredom for the sake of friendships she was developing.

"I'm just here to experience being in an Italian school," she said. "I can't speak Italian, so how can I take it more seriously? But I'll work harder, so I can stay."

She was able to talk during breaks in class, but she picked up a bad habit. Lucy and I were riding a city bus one day when we saw Suzye walk by with a cigarette in her mouth. We confronted her that evening.

"They smoke so much at school," she said. "During the five-minute breaks between classes, everyone goes outside and smokes. Everyone. Teachers, too."

We let her know we were disappointed in her choosing to smoke with her friends, but other than warning her of the dangers of getting addicted and of the health hazards, we knew we couldn't do anything to stop her when she was out of our sight. It hurt inside to see her reject the values we had tried to teach, but we also understood the strong pull of peer pressure and how important it was for her to feel part of the group.

There were other interesting differences at school as well.

"On people's birthdays, students bring in bottles of wine," Suzye said. "It's totally allowed. Nobody gets drunk or anything, not in school, not even out of school. But it's the weirdest thing to see students and teachers drinking alcohol together. If someone got caught with a bottle of wine in an American school, they'd be suspended."

Quite true, I knew from my years of teaching high school. Teachers and administrators wasted quite a bit of time policing the bathrooms and the nearby wooded areas to discourage smoking and drinking. It was nice to know that Italian teachers didn't have to waste time trying to bust students for these habits—but I hoped that my fifth graders wouldn't start bringing wine to class.

One thing the girls did like about Italy was the clothing, and they bought a lot during our stay. We encouraged this by bribing them to read classic works of English and American literature, which were available in the foreign language section of the bookstore Feltrinelli. For each book they finished, Lucy allotted a certain amount to their shopping budget, and they dug in enthusiastically. They were already avid readers, and so they were twice rewarded for their good habits.

"I do like this part of Italy," Suzye told me. She and Lindsey were trying on their latest purchases and posing for photos around the apartment, in the elevators and in the parks and piazzas.

"The shops here are so awesome," Lindsey said. "Look at this top. It buttons up the sides."

"So what are you doing with all the photos?" I asked.

"We send them to our friends back home," Suzye said. "Now they're way jealous of us."

We had Thanksgiving dinner with Stefano and Nancy and their three sons. Thanksgiving is not a holiday in Italy, but Nancy had taught her sons English, so it was a welcome cultural exchange for both families. Nancy roasted a turkey with dressing, and Lucy made two pies, pumpkin and walnut. She made the crust with oil, since she couldn't find shortening, and the pumpkin filling she made from scratch. She usually makes a Jell-O and fruit salad, but she couldn't find Jell-O or a substitute, so we had a plain fruit salad.

The dinner typified our growing comfort with life in Italy. We were all making friends in ways that blended our American habits with our new culture. We weren't exactly becoming Italians, but we were coping, adapting and growing comfortable. Italians were reaching out to us, and if both sides adjusted a little, we were meeting in the middle.

Chapter 14: Settling in at school

By now I had adjusted to the pace of my fifth-grade students, and they had adjusted to me. Of my fourteen students, ten were Italian, two American, one French and one was from Israel. I taught them English, history, art, science and information technology. I was also supposed to teach music, but I was able to pawn this off on Catherine, the other fifth-grade teacher, in exchange for doing some lessons for her class. My students took mathematics and physical education from two British teachers. The ten Italian students also went to Bruna several times a week for Italian grammar lessons, while the four *stranieri* a different teacher who helped them learn Italian.

During the hours my class went to other teachers, I team-taught the middle-school information technology classes in the computer lab, and I taught a journalism class to the eighth graders. I was also responsible for coordinating the first and probably only student newspaper the school ever had. Together with volunteers from the journalism class, we produced five editions of the *Corriere della Scuola*, a name suggested by one of the students because of the name similarity with the national newspaper *Corriere della Sera.*

I enjoyed being able to teach more advanced skills to the middle-schoolers, but I was most at home with my fifth-graders. In the British system, elementary students call their teachers by first name, and so they did at EISP. I had no problem adjusting to this, but one of my American students,

Ryan, couldn't get used to it and decided out of respect to call me Mr. Paul. The others all called me Pōl, with just a trace of a vowel sound at the end—not quite Pōl-uh, but almost.

Ryan impressed everyone by his quick adaptation into the Italian culture and language, while my other American student, whom I will call Norma, proved to be somewhat of a challenge. About a month into the school year, she developed crying fits during school, for reasons that remained a mystery. She said she was sick and wanted to go home, but she had no physical symptoms.

I spoke to Norma several times in private but couldn't coax any logical explanation out of her. She was doing well in her schoolwork. She was a bit of a loner, the kind of child who seems more comfortable talking to adults than with fellow students. However, the others were always polite to her and didn't seem to exclude her. She had been in the same class the previous year. Did she do this last year? Yes, she said, sometimes.

She just needed some time out to compose herself, so I would let her use the bathroom and then she would come back and make it through the day. I tried to give her some extra attention, and she would go several days without any problems, but just when it seemed that we had put her bouts of anxiety to rest, she would have another breakdown. Her parents were not without sympathy, but they were also mystified by Norma's behavior. We shared strategies on how to help her, but one morning she came out of the bathroom after a bout of crying and told me she was sick, had thrown up and wanted me to call her parents to pick her up. I had my doubts that she had really thrown up, but I didn't want to upset her more by questioning her veracity.

It was almost lunch time, so I told her I would ask Angela to call her parents to come get her. Angela demonstrated once again why she had been picked over me to head the elementary school. We called Norma over to our table to tell her story again.

Even though I witnessed it first hand, I still can't describe how Angela did it. She was soothing and sympathetic, but then she said, "You didn't really throw up in the bathroom, did you, Norma?"

"Well, I kind of choked a little bit . . . no, I didn't throw up," Norma confessed. "Let's not tell my parents about this, okay?" And somehow, that was the end of Norma's crying.

The fact that most of my students were Italian didn't advance my language learning one bit, because they were not allowed to speak Italian at school. If they didn't understand an English word, I was not supposed to give them the Italian equivalent or ask another student to supply the Italian word. Only English words could be used to explain the meaning.

I did learn a few spontaneous utterances that stuck with me. When one kid was annoying another, I would hear, "*Smettila!*" Stop it! "*Sbrigati!*" Hurry up! Or "*Stai zitto!*" a cross between shut up and be quiet, depending on how it is said. Something disgusting always elicited, "*Che schifo!*" I also learned a little about Italian sentence structure by the way the children phrased their answers. "Whose pen is this?" I asked while picking up a pen from the floor. "It is of Anna," I was told. Etienne once complained, "Marco *superated* me," when Marco moved ahead of him in line. Ah, *superare* mean "to pass," I thought, and I have remembered that word ever since. I also fondly remember Suzye's Erica calling our home and using her best English but still retaining an Italian structure: "I am Erica. Eez there Suzye?" I thought this so endearing that I never told her it is more common to say, "This is Erica. Is Suzye there?"

I had come to Italy speaking more Italian than my family, but at the rate I was going, my family would soon *superate* . I tried to squeeze in some learning on weekends, but much of my time was occupied with lesson planning and grading. We tried to speak Italian at home but didn't get far because we had important topics to discuss and could only speak Italian in simple phrases and sentences. The girls were becoming happier, but they occasionally felt homesick and had crying spells, and they still pushed against the limits imposed on them. Our family structure required as much sensitivity as possible to remain strong, and we couldn't afford to sacrifice meaningful communication for the sake of greater linguistic skills.

Chapter 14: Adventures and misadventures

Christmas break was on its way, and Lucy and I spent some time on the Internet at my school making plans for a trip to Austria and Germany. But first, we would be spending time in Padova with our family—everyone! Our son, Randy, would be flying in from Singapore December 18, and Sandy on December 23, so our whole family would be together.

We had experienced a few misadventures on trains and buses already. Once we had planned a trip to Venezia, but I put us on a train to Firenze, which went the opposite direction. After a few stops, I realized that the cities we were passing through were south of Padova, not east.

"The word Venezia sounds a little like Firenze, doesn't it?" I said to Lucy.

"No, not much," she said. "Maybe a little, I guess. Why?"

"Because I think I put us on the wrong train. We need to get off."

"I thought something seemed different," she said. "But you seemed so sure."

Suzye and Lindsey were oblivious. I think I could have just told them it was time to switch trains and they never would have realized I had made a mistake. Unfortunately, Lucy tattled on me, so now they had something to tease me about.

December, though, was to be a peak month for transportation problems.

First, Lucy and I took the wrong bus to meet Randy and his friend Sumay (who would be visiting for just a couple of days) at the airport near Venezia. It was a local bus, taking a round-about route through every little city on the way. Padova to Venezia is only a half hour by train, but the train doesn't go to the airport, so we figured we'd just do it all with one bus. However, we made so many stops and the traffic was so bad that we weren't even half way there when the plane landed.

"How much longer until Venezia?" I asked the driver.

"*Dipende*," he said, shrugging. "I can't control the traffic." We arrived a full hour and a half late, and in Venezia instead of the airport in Tessera, on the mainland. We had obviously misunderstood the directions we'd received at the Padova bus station about which bus to take.

We also hadn't brought Randy's cell phone number with us, so we had to wait until Suzye got home from school so we could call her and ask her to find the number and give it to us. When we finally reached Randy and Sumay by phone, we told them to take a taxi and meet us in Venezia. At least from there we'd know how to take a train back to Padova.

But since we were in *La Serenissima*, the most serene and famous city of canals and bridges, when Randy and Sumay arrived, we decided to stroll a little before taking the train. Randy and I separated from the ladies and got lost. We knew we had to get across the Canal Grande, but we couldn't find a bridge. We kept running down little lanes that came right up to the canal but offered no way to cross.

"We just need to be right over there," I said, pointing to the sidewalk on the opposite shore. "It's so close. But I don't think I can jump fifty feet."

"Where's a gondola when we need one, Dad?" Randy said.

When we finally arrived at the station, we had missed what we thought was the last train that evening. Then we heard that a train for Nizza was late but was about to depart. Where is Nizza, we wondered? Nice, France, someone told us, so we jumped on, knowing that Padova was on the way and only a half hour west of Venezia. It was good to get home; Venezia is cold in December, and so were we.

More misadventures awaited us with Sandy's scheduled arrival. She had narrowly missed a connection deadline and ended up routed to Frankfurt, Germany, instead of Milano, Italy. She tried to take a long series of trains through Germany and Austria that would bring her to Padova at 3:55 a.m. on December 24, after nine different connections. One train broke down, though, spoiling the schedule, but we wouldn't learn this until later. Lucy and I went to meet her at the station, and when she didn't get off the 3:55 a.m. train, I asked the conductor if I could take a quick pass through the train to see if she was aboard but sleeping. He said okay, but I didn't find her. When the next train pulled in, I tried the same thing. This time I didn't ask the conductor, and the train took off with me still aboard! It was an express train, too, so I had to go all the way to Rovigo, twenty minutes away. Then I had to get off, wait outside the closed station in the early-morning chill for a train to pass in the opposite direction, and get back on—all of this with no ticket. I explained myself to the conductor on the first train, but I didn't want to try again on the second train, so I hid in the bathroom for most of the trip back. I could have bought a ticket on board for an extra fee, but I figured I had already paid a premium price in wasted time and frozen fingers for my stupidity. Lucy, by this time, had given up and gone home.

"Did you have a nice trip?" she asked when I walked in the door. "And why didn't you bring Sandy with you?"

"Very funny. And yes, I did have a nice trip. I went all the way to Firenze this time and helped them put up the Christmas lights on the statue of David."

"Oh, by the way, Sandy called from Bolzano to say she's been given a new arrival time of noon. Do you think you could go meet her, but maybe this time wait until she actually gets off the train?"

Sandy would make it in time for Christmas Eve, at least. Italy would be so much nicer if we could teleport all of our family and friends there! We spent a relaxing Christmas day listening to music, talking, opening presents and feasting on a dinner made mostly by Lucy. That evening I went to the train station with Sandy and Lucy to plan an adventure for the following day. We decided to go to Trieste and then see if we could go across the border into Slovenia.

It drizzled steadily during our trip, but it was so pleasant to doze and chat in the gently rocking train. We made it into Sežana in Slovenia, but then what? We had no plans, and now it was raining hard, so walking around the somewhat grubby little town didn't appeal to us. A man in the bar said we could hire a car and go see the famous Lipizzaner horses or the Škocjan Caves. By unanimous verdict, we chose the caves, which were only fifteen minutes away and kept us out of the rain while enjoying the beauty of spectacular stalactites, stalagmites and limestone pools in what is reputed to be the world's largest underground canyon. At one point we were told the parking lot was 450 feet above our heads.

After returning to Padova, we rented a car for a few days later and went up into the Dolomiti Mountains near Asiago, where Randy, Lindsey and I rented equipment and had a great time skiing on the machine-made snow. Suzye rented snowboarding equipment and set off on her own.

"Seven minutes," Randy said. "The crowd is so small that we made it up the lift and back down again in seven minutes." We didn't see much of Suzye, though. We found out later she had fallen on the ice and hit her head and spent most of her day in the lodge. She had fully recovered by the end of the day, though. Lucy and Sandy spent the time in Bassano del Grappa and Nove, shopping for gifts and decorations for Sandy's coming July wedding. When we returned to Padova, we celebrated Suzye's seventeenth birthday and Lindsey's fifteenth, both of which occurred in late December.

Randy and Sandy left the next day, and then we spent the next couple of days resting and making plans for our most elaborate trip of the school year. We forgot to eat lentils and wear red underwear for good luck on New Year's Eve, Italian traditions. Instead Lucy and I went to church and prayed and sang with friends. Afterward, we walked home and watched fireworks of all sizes and types, which were much the same as we would see in an American city on this night. Earlier that evening, Steve had told us of his years in Rome in the eighties, where the celebrations were less restrained.

"People on their porches were setting fireworks off, and you had to be alert so you didn't get lit up by a stray rocket," he said. "Parked cars ended up with scorched spots on them either from fireworks raining down from above or people using the cars to light their fireworks on."

Before he came to Italy, it had been even more dangerous because of a tradition of "out with the old and in with the new," he said. "People would throw their old furniture off their balconies and everybody below had to look out." Apparently this still happens in a few places in the South, but the tradition never made it to Padova.

With Randy and Sandy gone and the holidays nearly over, Suzye and Lindsey grew bitterly homesick again, and they begged us once more to send them home to live with their friends. Suzye seemed especially depressed, and I heard her crying in her bedroom and went in to talk to her.

"We've been here long enough," she whimpered. "I miss my friends so much. I'd just be so much happier back in Gig Harbor."

"You're going to live to be ninety years old," I said. "Six more months is only about $1/140^{th}$ of your life. In the grand scheme of things, that's not much."

"No, I'm missing one fourth of the best years of my life," she countered.

I could have countered that high school may not *really* be the best years of one's life, but I didn't want to go off on a tangent. However, I had little to say that would convince her. How does a dad say gently, "I don't want you doing any more stupid things that might mess up your life," or "You'll regret even more missing out on one of the best years of your life if you leave now"?

Suzye and Lindsey's periodic outbursts made me feel terrible—because it was my dream to come to Italy, and I had forced them to come with me. If I had waited four more years, the girls would have been in college and independent. Instead, our relationship was strained, but I knew it was not in their best interests to send them back, so I prayed that they would resolve to make the best of the experience and use it to grow instead of becoming despondent and bitter.

"You know," I ventured. "You've lived your entire lives in one house. You've known most of your friends since elementary school; you've never had to leave your comfort zones and reach out to make new friends.

"I understand this because I was the same way growing up, and I remember how difficult it was for me to leave my shell when I went off to college. I didn't have experience making new friends, because if the new kids in school wanted me for a friend, they always had to reach out to me. They had to ask me questions about myself. It took me years to realize that I had missed out on learning the social skills needed to make new friends. You girls have a chance to learn that lesson in high school."

Friends had told me that by the end of the year, my daughters would be thanking me for bringing them to Italy, but in January, I began to seriously doubt this.

Since my school didn't reopen until January 7, Lucy, Suzye, Lindsey and I boarded a train January first and headed for Innsbruck, Austria. Even when we were only a half hour across the border, we immediately noticed the stark differences. The streets were wide, clean and smooth instead of a mishmash of broken and uneven bricks or pot-holed pavement. The buildings were old, but none of them were falling apart. Pedestrians obeyed the "don't walk" signs, and the crosswalks tweeted pleasantly to assist blind people to cross. Buses and trains were newer and cleaner. As much as Italy had charmed us, Lucy and I realized that, like Suzye and Lindsey, we also missed the security of a predictable country with a more modern infrastructure.

Poor Suzye came down with a fever on the journey and missed a day of skiing and snowboarding on some fantastically fresh Alpine powder. She also missed a trip to see the Disney-like Neuschwanstein Castle in Hohenschwangau.

After two days in Innsbruck, Suzye had recovered and we caught a train to Munich and then on to Dachau to visit the first German concentration camp. We learned that the camp was made to hold 5,000 prisoners but often had held 12,000, and that estimates of those who died there ranged from 32,000 to 35,000. About a third of the inmates were Jewish, but the prison also held Catholic priests, communists, homosexuals, convicted criminals, Jehovah's Witnesses, mentally handicapped people and prisoners of war from Russia, Poland, France and Yugoslavia. Being there in the dead of winter, even dressed in our heavy winter clothes, gave us great empathy for the condition of the poor souls who had to endure imprisonment in only their flimsy prison uniforms. We were shaking and our feet were numb by the end of the tour, but we had no regrets about coming. It was a sight and feeling that will stay with us forever, made all the more real knowing that Lucy had ancestors who were Dutch Jewish. Lucy still has contact with her relatives in the Netherlands, and they have told her that some members of the Bonnist family died in prisons during the war for the offense of being of Jewish origin.

On a less serious note, at the train station in Munich, Lucy had to use the bathroom, which was staffed by an attendant who collected a user fee. The rates and descriptions were in German, of course, and it seemed that everyone ahead of her in line was paying the higher price of 1.10 euro. Always on the lookout for a bargain, Lucy asked if she could go the budget route and just pay the .60 euro listed for the "*pissoir.*" She received an odd look, then a smile and a shake of the head. "For men," the attendant said, and Lucy had to fork out the full amount. I told her later she should have stood up for her rights and not take such sexist discrimination sitting down, but I think by that time she understood and accepted the situation.

Lindsey also used the facilities, and we waited an exceptionally long time for her to come out.

"Everything okay?" Lucy asked her when she returned.

"The bathrooms are so much cleaner and prettier than in Italy," Lindsey explained. "After paying so much, I wanted to get my money's worth."

Overall the trip probably made the girls more homesick than they were before, because the farther north we went, the more modern everything looked. Houses, streets, sidewalks, technology—everything seemed newer, bigger, cleaner, more efficient. The grocery stores had more American products, and the shelves and goods were not so tightly packed together. Even the teenagers looked more American, being a mixture of blonds and brunettes instead of 90 percent dark haired. Suzye and Lindsey both immediately commented that they liked German and Austrian guys better, even though they had only actually talked to one young Austrian.

"They don't spike their hair with a lot of grease," Suzye said. "They look more normal, not so disco-y."

"They wear normal pants and shoes, not tight, distressed denim and pointy shoes," Lindsey said. "It also seems so much safer in the train stations. There's a cafe open in the middle of the night with a television playing. In Italy, it feels dangerous for a girl to be stuck in a train station late at night. It's hard to find a place to sit, and guys harass us."

I think the girls were wondering why we had gone to Italy instead of Germany or Austria. To them, modernity was synonymous with superiority, and being as thoroughly American as I was, I couldn't help but be pestered with the same thoughts. It was darned frustrating to walk five blocks in Padova to pick up some groceries only to realize for perhaps the tenth time that this little local store was closed every Wednesday afternoon and I'd have to walk five blocks back home.

As far as scenic beauty went, the snow-covered Bavarian villages comprised the most beautiful vistas we'd seen anywhere in the world. From what we could see, the people were just as friendly as the Italians. We also noticed that more people spoke English here—not just in the tourism industry but everyday people we met in stores, buses and trains. Conversely, the German language baffled us. The words were so long and unfamiliar that we were forever forgetting the names of bus and metro stops. When someone tells you to get off at *Giotto*—an Italian street in Padova—it's so much easier to remember than *Zweibrückenstraße*.

I had to remind myself that I had come to Italy to get a glimpse of the old country while it still retained some of the characteristics and qualities of my grandfather's time. Someday, Italy will be as modern as Germany and America. Someday Southern Italy will be as modern as Northern Italy, and Slovenia will be as modern as Italy. Eventually, English will be spoken everywhere and stores will be open twenty-four hours a day. In the meantime, we had a chance to see a little of what life was like before globalization did its thing, and this opportunity wouldn't be available when the girls were my age. We had a chance to view an image—admittedly fading quickly—of the Italy that *Nonno* and *Nonna* had experienced—with tiny butcher shops, bakeries and farmers' markets still active in every little neighborhood. As we took the train back toward Padova, I watched the landscape change from tall, jagged white Alps to the lower, worn-out looking Dolomites, a much older mountain range. The cities seemed to reflect the changing mountains. Austrian homes were white stucco and wood with brown trim; the buildings were tall, with narrow church spires. The Italian buildings were older, grayer and—like the Dolomites—crumbling. The valleys were tapestried with ancient vineyards and the hillsides with stone terraces and olive trees. Here the *contadini* still survived by sweat, strain and working the soil using the techniques of their ancestors. Our trip to Germany and Austria helped me to remember my purpose for having come to Italy, and if anything, it made me want to go farther south, where life was even slower, more like it had been when my grandparents left a hundred years ago.

Chapter 15: Blundering along with good humor

After our vacation, Lucy and Lindsey continued in their classes at the Bertrand Russell language school. One of the nice features of the language school was after-hours activities, and one of the most memorable was the Montefortiana walking marathon in Monteforte d'Alpone near Soave. We had to be at the school at Sunday at 6:30 a.m. We weren't told where we were going or why—just that we would be gone all day, to wear comfortable shoes and clothes and to dress warmly, but in layers. Suzye didn't make it out of bed, but Lucy and Lindsey and I were ready to go. For us and all but a handful of people, it was just a hike in the hills—though we all registered, paid a fee and were given numbers to put on our shirts as if we were really racing. We also got fed after signing up: fruit, cake, cookies, bread and boiled eggs, along with wine and tea. A little farther along, we stopped for sausage and more wine and tea. I never knew marathons could be so rewarding!

Once out of the city, we hiked the dirt trail in small groups through gorgeous undulating hills covered with grape vines and olive trees. Our escorts from the school spoke Italian with us as we walked. At a certain point, the trail branched in two directions. To the right was the nine-kilometer course; the left trail took a fourteen-kilometer route. Lindsey had been walking slightly ahead of us and came upon it first, and she harkened unto the famous words of baseball player Yogi Berra, who advised: "When you come to a fork in the road, take it." Actually, she didn't even look up and notice there was a fork. She had what I can only describe as a "Lindsey moment" and didn't notice the trail had divided. She just followed some people walking ahead of her and ended up taking the long route. The rest of our group came to the fork and reached an agreement to take the shorter route, and we could only hope that Lindsey had chosen it as well and would eventually stop to wait for us. She did stop later to wait for us, but of course we never came, leaving her to wonder if we had somehow passed her without her noticing. Then she spent the rest of the time trying to catch up to us. We didn't see her again until a good half hour after we had finished the course, and naturally forever after she was teased about her solo *passeggiata* whenever the opportunity presented itself.

More prizes awaited us after the marathon: tortellini and a box of wine, oil, juice and a beach towel. I had an embarrassing moment when the language school group went off to buy gelato while I stood watching everyone's boxes. A group of smiling Italian men passed by and made some comments about how many prizes I had won. I smiled back, not knowing exactly what they had said but getting the general concept. Then one man said something about that being too many prizes for one person, and he would help me out by taking some off my hands. He picked up a couple of the boxes and started walking away, looking over his shoulder and smiling, waiting for me to protest. I knew this was the place where I was supposed to say something clever, like . . . Well, I couldn't even think of something clever to say in English, let alone Italian, so I just stood there like an idiot, grinning foolishly. I tried to look confident in the knowledge that this was just a joke and he would return the prizes any second now. He kept getting farther away, waiting for me to say something, but my brain utterly failed me. All I could think of is how I would explain to the other language students why two boxes were missing. Fortunately, the man returned with the boxes, probably feeling bad for trying to steal from a feeble-minded, deaf-mute man. To this day I still feel foolish for not being able to say anything more than "Grazie."

Though our language skills were advancing and we felt proud that we were able to shop and travel, we had other moments of utter confusion. Riding the bus home from school one day, I embarrassed myself by misunderstanding a lady who sat in the empty seat next to me. A few seconds after she sat down, she said something with *"posto"* at the end of the sentence. One of the lines in my Italian textbook had the phrase, *"È occupato, questo posto?"* which means, "Is this seat occupied?" Thinking that must be what she said, I replied, "No." She gave me a funny look and then spoke to a man standing next to her, saying essentially the same thing. He said yes, and she got up and went to talk to a woman friend a few seats ahead of us. Then she came back and sat in the empty seat next to me, and by this time I realized that she had said, *"Puo salvare questo posto?"* I had rudely but unintentionally refused to save her seat for her. I was able to apologize and showed her the vocabulary flash cards that at that moment I had in my hands because I was *"imparando Italiano,"* learning Italian. We were both able to smile at my blunder, and I was grateful for the chance to explain myself.

Telling this story a few days later to Steve and Patti, they laughed politely and looked at each other knowingly.

"That's nothing compared to what happened to our friend Terry when he was riding on a bus," Steve said. "He had come to Italy to be a missionary, but first he had to take language classes, and he had some pitfalls along the way. You know that to say you like something in Italian, you should say, '*Mi piace*' or '*Mi piacciono,*' don't you?"

"Yes," I replied, "I know that p*iacere* means 'to please,' so saying '*mi piace*' literally means 'it pleases me,' and '*mi piacciono*' means 'they please me.' "

"Right, and how do you say you're sorry?"

"It's almost the same," I answered. "You just change *piace* to *dispiace*, as in 'it displeases me,' which is what Italians say to apologize."

"Right again. So Terry was riding standing up on a very crowded bus, which made a sudden lurch, causing him to stumble headfirst in the chest of a buxom Italian woman. And guess what he blurted out: '*Mi piace, mi piace!*' instead of '*Mi dispiace.*' "

"Hah," I laughed. "Probably a Freudian slip. But then, maybe he should have said, '*Mi piacciono*' instead."

"You also need to be extra careful when using certain words," Patti cautioned. "Mispronouncing *penne* as *pene* is the difference between a type of pasta and a penis. *Anno* is year, while *ano* is anus. *Fico* means fig, and it is also slang for cool, trendy or a sexy guy. But *fica* is a crude word for female genitalia."

These similar sounding words reminded Steve of another story.

"Another missionary had a terrible experience the first time he preached in Italian," Steve said. "The gist of his message was that we should not be discouraged. But there are only a few subtle differences between *scoraggiare*, discourage, and *scorregiare*, which means to pass gas. He repeatedly used the wrong word, and hence he essentially preached that his listeners should not fart."

"Actually," Patti said, "That's pretty good advice in a land where *fare la bella figura* (to make a good impression) is important, but not exactly a message with the spiritual significance he intended."

"Now I try at all costs to never use the Italian word discouragement," Steve said, "because after hearing that story, I can never quite be positive that the correct word is going to come out of my mouth."

Okay, and now I never want to ask for *penne* pasta, wish anyone a *buon capodanno* or call anyone *figa*—or was that supposed to be *figo?*—ever again.

Chapter 16: Wine, women and aggressive males

A different type of lost in translation moment occurred the next week, when Lucy and Lindsey's language school hosted a dinner for all the students at the home of the director, Cristina. She had designed her house with a long room that also served as a kitchen so that large groups could dine while she cooked for them. She invited some of her Italian friends so the students could practice their conversation skills with native speakers. It seemed like a nice idea, with great food, wine, company and conversation. Suzye and Lindsey sat at the other end of the table, and unbeknownst to us, Suzye had been enthusiastically helping herself to the plentiful bottles of wine. Lucy discovered Suzye acting strangely in the bathroom and called me. When I came, Suzye was propped against the wall inside the bathroom with her lip split from having fallen against the toilet. She was muttering about stupid Italians who drink too much wine. She had trouble standing up, and Lindsey, who had been drinking Coca-Cola, thought it was all very amusing. One of the other students told me some people at the table had urged Suzye to drink more. "*Sono cattivi amici,*" they are bad friends, he said.

We encouraged Suzye to throw up in the toilet, but she didn't want to. An Italian who had a car drove Suzye and me home, but not before Suzye deposited most of her wine and dinner in the backseat of his car, and on her clothes and mine. We apologized repeatedly, but the driver was very gracious about the whole thing. Who knows, maybe he was one of those who encouraged Suzye to drink more and got what he deserved. I was also sorry for Suzye, whose first chance to sample the fine wines of Italy ended in such a public disaster.

Sobered up the following morning, she explained that she had never been intoxicated before.

"They had that sparkling wine that didn't even taste alcoholic," she said. "And then the Canadian girl kept bringing bottles down to our end of the table."

"Well, now you have some motivation not to do it again," I said. "You made a fine mess of Alfiero's car—not to mention your shirt and my jeans."

"Who's Alfiero? The last thing I remember is Mom asking me if I was drunk, and I said, 'No, I'm okay,' and then I stumbled back against the wall, fell and hit my head on the toilet and broke my braces. I don't remember anything after that."

I felt some relief to know that this was the first time she had been drunk. I couldn't have said the same thing to my parents when I was seventeen. Okay, I could have, but not truthfully.

Overall, the tight quarters of our apartment helped bring our family closer together. We played Scrabble and did jigsaw puzzles, things we had rarely done in the last couple of years. Even when we just quietly sat and read, we were no more than one room away, so we talked more than we had in our huge American house. The girls continued seeing the friends they'd made in the Italian school, so they were busy and gradually adjusting to their new lives.

One thing that continued to bother us was how late they stayed out with their friends. Even though we were getting to know and trust Erica more, we still worried. The various dance clubs they attended required them to take late night and then early morning trains and buses. We bought them cheap cell phones so they could call us if they were in any trouble. They reassured us that they were careful and felt safe—but would they really tell us if they weren't, knowing that we would likely restrict their freedom?

"Don't you run into guys who try to take advantage of you?" Lucy asked. She spoke from her own experience, because she had encountered an aggressive man in Bassano del Grappa. She had stopped at a bakery to ask for directions, and the young man at the counter referred her to a customer in his sixties who spoke some English and said he could help her.

However, the old man was not about to give the directions without asking for a little something in return. He tried to hold her hand, but Lucy pulled it away. He tried again several times without success, and then he asked her to sit and have tea with him. His speech was slurred and mixed with profanities, and Lucy smelled liquor on his breath. She kept asking for the directions she needed, but he kept delaying. He began telling her about himself. He was a *professore* from India who took care of disabled children. He loved his children and would do anything for them. Lucy looked pleadingly at the bakery employee, who seemed sympathetic and a bit exasperated. He spoke to the man and tried to get him to just give the directions. Lucy was perhaps too patient and polite, but she continued to pull her hand away, interrupt and ask for directions. The professore finally forgot about his charm, grabbed her hand again and told her to shut up. She pulled her hand away for the last time and walked off as his angry denunciations followed her out the door.

Suzye assured us that most of the time when they were approached, it was in tourist areas such as the train or bus stations, and the guys rarely did anything more than persistently try to make conversation.

"They usually start out with '*Ciao, bella,*' and move on to other questions that we don't always understand," she said. "When they figure out we're not Italian, they move on to 'You speak French? You speak English? Oh, you want a coffee? You are so beautiful. I love you. I must see you again, baby.' "

"At first we thought it was just from Italian boys, but we get hit on more aggressively from immigrants hanging around the train station," Lindsey added. "The boys at the Italian school don't talk like this at all."

It seems that foreign girls were usually the targets, and if boys didn't know they were outsiders, the girls had little to worry about.

"It was kind of a novelty at first," Suzye said, "and we played along to see what else the boys would say. However, they don't know much English, and it gets boring. We had to learn how to avoid being approached. We just don't look at them in the first place. If you give them eye contact, then they'll talk to you. If you walk confidently and just look at the ground, they won't approach you. And if they do, even if it's just innocent questions like where are you from, we don't answer because they'll think we're interested and will keep asking more questions."

Lindsey said she made up a story that she had used more than once. "I say my name is Miya and I'm from New York and that I don't remember my phone number. The last part is actually true."

"I found another solution," Suzye said. "Now I ask for their phone numbers instead. Then they feel like they've accomplished something."

Lindsey smiled, adding, "Remember that guy who said, 'I'm waiting for your call, beautiful' when we walked away? Then I started trying that too. It worked great, especially with that guy who couldn't find a piece of paper to write down his number. He finally took out some money and wrote it on that."

"Anyhow, Erica watches out for us," Suzye said. "She can tell us what the guys are saying. Sometimes she pretends to be a foreign student, too. We were having tea with some guys, and they were trying out their English lines on us. But then they'd talk among themselves in Italian, not knowing that Erica could understand everything. She said one of them made a really rude comment, and then she shocked them when she told them to buzz off—in Italian, of course."

I never got to witness any of these incidents in person, except for one memorable occasion in February when I turned into a raging papa bear. We were returning from a day trip to Treviso on a train, and Suzye and Lindsey sat about three seats away from us. The seats directly across from them became vacant at one of the stops, and three high-school-aged boys came down the aisle, sat down and tried to engage the girls in conversation. They seemed nice enough, but one in particular was persistent and fairly aggressive. The girls were politely saying no thanks to the boys. Lucy and I watched with some amusement, but then the lead boy reached out and put his hand on Suzye's knee while continuing to talk.

This dad had watched long enough—I stood and spoke loudly and firmly, *"Basta! Non toccare!"* I wanted to say more, but my language skills were too limited. Naturally I didn't want to admit this, so I just remained standing and gave the boys what I hoped was a withering glare. The offending boy let loose a stream of apologetic Italian, something about only trying to be friendly and not meaning any harm, I think. I had no words to add, so I just continued to look stern while the boys moved on to the next car.

Later I thought of something I could have said, but that's pretty much the way it went whenever I tried to speak Italian. I always thought of something better to say five minutes after the conversation ended. Anyway, I was pleased as it was that I had managed, "Enough! You're not to touch!" so convincingly that the boy must have thought I was Italian. But I wish I had added, *"Potete parlare, ma non toccare."* You can talk but not touch.

Author and cultural sociologist Roger Friedland has written that American and Italian women are equally likely to endure harassment, but the Italian version is safer. While living in Rome with his two teen daughters, Friedland observed that young women frequently walked alone at night in Rome's city center, waiting near midnight for the last buses home. As a professor who studies and teaches about love, sex and God, he asked the women in his class if they were harassed or afraid. They told him that boys routinely made unwanted remarks, came too close and sometimes touched them where they didn't want to be touched. However, the women were not afraid. Although women in both countries were harassed, Friedland wrote in his book, *Amore*: "There is a difference, a big one: American men are much more likely to commit rape. One-quarter of female college students in America will experience either rape or attempted rape. Twelve percent of high school girls have already been raped. The real numbers are likely much higher, because many women not only don't tell the police; they don't tell anyone."

Friedland said his Italian students were stunned to hear these statistics. Fewer than 5 percent of Italian women between the ages of sixteen and twenty-four have ever experienced rape or attempted rape. Most of that—about 70 percent—was committed by their intimate partner.

"The question is, why?" Friedland asks. "It's not because Roman men don't look. They are voracious with their eyes, savoring the bodies of women as they pass. After all the time I've spent in Rome, I've come to think that part of the reason rape is so much rarer in Italy is that Italian men love women more than American men do. Beneath all the sexual jest, the lusty looks and suggestive remarks, Roman men respect women."

Friedland's daughters were subjected to harassment in Rome, but they learned to cope along with the Italian girls. He said that Italians accept that flirting is part of human nature but is not a precursor to rape. Girls in Italy are free to "swear at the boys, to berate them, hit them on the heads or in the face, belittling them for their pathetic antics." His girls didn't regard the advances as dangerous.

"Roman women who grow up in the system learn to maneuver, to parry and resist the verbal and visual predations of men, because they feel relatively safe from violation," he writes. "Roman girls learn early not to be afraid of boys. They grow accustomed to walking alone to the square to fetch olive oil or pizza bianca for their mothers."

Friedland also contrasted Americans and Italians in their beliefs about marriage. The American students he surveyed while teaching at UC Santa Barbara wondered whether love is real; they seemed afraid to believe in love and lifelong marriage because they had witnessed so much disappointment in their parents' relationships. Only about 60 percent of the UC students said they wanted to marry and stay with one person all their lives, and less than half said they actually expected to.

And why should they? Of American couples who married in the first five years of the 1990s, 42 percent divorced within fifteen years. By contrast, only 8 percent of comparable Italian couples had separated. In the United States, close to half of all marriages are remarriages. In Italy, 95 percent of all marriages are first-time ventures for both parties.

Friedland also found that Italians are—to put it delicately—better lovers. To put it less delicately, he said, "Young Italians—especially females, but also males—have more frequent orgasms than young Americans. Love makes for pleasure. Love radically increases the probability that a woman will have an orgasm. Italians still revere passion. Because the men love the women, they are more likely to care about giving them pleasure. And the women they love take pleasure from that love. Men's love works."

Again, the question must be asked, why this difference? The heart of the answer has to do with how Italians experience family and family life. Italian families are all-absorbing, involving grandparents, cousins, aunts and uncles.

"Roman kids are deeply invested in their families—forever," he said. "Unlike middle-class American kids, who leave for college and return home just to rest and refuel, most young Italians continue to live at home while attending university. When Roman kids do move out, it's to get married and set up their own households. That often happens nearby, even in the very same building their parents live in, frequently with their parents help. And overwhelmingly, they rely on their parents to care for their children when they can't be there."

As far as our own experiences go, we saw husbands and wives yelling at each other on the streets, families arguing loudly in houses as we passed by, and we read headlines in the newspapers about murder and abuse. We've also been warned that certain parts of large cities are unsafe to walk in at night. But to fear, as I did a few years before, that Italy may be more dangerous for my daughters than the United States was nonsense—unless I was worried that they might fall in love and have stable marriages.

Suzye and Lindsey agreed that they were approached in Italy more often than in America, but they said they hadn't felt seriously threatened and were always able to walk away. Dressing modestly but also somewhat stylishly will make foreigners blend in more with the Italian women, Lindsey advised: "I found that if I dress poorly—baggy pants, no makeup, unstyled hair—harassment is worse. It seems to go against logic, but perhaps I seemed more attainable."

Travelers could also learn a few Italian phrases, such as *vai via* (go away) or *mi lascia in pace* (leave me alone, or literally, leave me in peace). As a last resort, one can make a scene, as I did on the train.

Chapter 17: Freedom to explore Italian roots

During one delicious week in February, I had the chance to travel entirely on my own, with no responsibilities or agenda. It was "white week" at my school—a midwinter vacation to give people a week off, presumably to visit white-capped mountains—but the rest of my family didn't have the week off. I took a train to Tuscany with no firm plans. I wanted to have some time to write, explore and meet Italians. Vacations were almost the only time I could advance my slowly developing language skills. I picked the region of Toscana because it would be warmer than the north but not too far to go in a short time. My heart soared as I boarded the train. I had married during my senior year of college; then I secured a steady job and had four children. This was the first time since college that I felt so much freedom!

I had picked out Cecina on the west coast of southern Toscana as a destination for at least a day or two, but on the train, I realized that with a short detour, I could pass through Pescia, the city listed on my grandfather's birth certificate. I had yet to visit the city. My cousin Enrico had obtained the birth certificate a few years prior and mailed it to me so I could start the process of my Italian citizenship.

Pescia is definitely not a tourist town. No taxis waited outside the station. No hotels were near the station. Even the two teenagers I spoke to in the parking lot across from the station looked puzzled when I asked where I could find a hotel *di buon prezzo*. Okay, how about a hotel of any price? One had no idea, but the other thought I would find one in the *centro* if I went down *"questa strada, e poi a sinistra."* Some other pedestrians later confirmed I was on the right street, and a mile and a half later I came to the Hotel dei Fiori. The first word that comes to mind when trying to describe Pescia is gritty—not in a negative sense, but the way movie critics describe a film as gritty when it portrays life as it truly is, without false distortions, stylization or idealizations— reminiscent of the neoclassical films of Federico Fellini. The main piazza looked like it hadn't changed much in the past hundred years, so I could imagine my *nonno* as one of the old men clustered on the sidewalks and talking about nothing in particular. I didn't know it at the time, but my *nonno* probably didn't spend a lot of time here, because I discovered a few years later that he was born near the train station and then his family moved a few miles west to San Salvatore during his teen years. Still, he undoubtedly had been here in the piazza, and so had his father and mother, as this was the focal point of the city.

Next I had to make it to Montecarlo to find the marriage certificate for Michele Spadoni and Anita Seghieri, something else I needed for my citizenship application. For that, I took a taxi, as I was told that Montecarlo was on a hilltop about ten minutes away with no train or bus service. If I loved Pescia for its grittiness, I immediately fell for the beauty of Montecarlo. With vineyards below and olive trees on the side hills, it is perched about 500 feet above the surrounding plains with a 300-degree view of the Valdinievole—the valley of the Nievole River—including Pescia to the north, Montecatini Alto to the east and all the way to Lucca on the west. It was ancient yet clean and compact, with a huge fortress and a tall church tower. I found an inscription on one building indicating that the houses on the main street had been built in the 1300s. In the central piazza, I found a memorial to soldiers and civilians who died in the wars, and among the fallen were several members of the Seghieri family—a discovery that made me feel sad for their families, and yet gratified because it added to my feeling that this is the place where I was from—my cousins had given their lives for this country. After I had found my grandparents' marriage certificate in the *municipio*, I strolled around the town, letting my imagination roam. Had Michele and Anita taken this same lane as they talked about their future together? They had married in Montecarlo on November 7, 1908. Could those pale-leafed trees with the gnarled, twisted trunks on the hillside have been part of the Seghieri family's olive groves?

While I had ostensibly begun seeking my Italian citizenship for the practical reason of being able to travel and work in the country freely, here I was in Italy, already able to do that. I think a truer, more pure reason for my desire—and the reason I was still seeking citizenship—is that I wanted an official document confirming that I belonged here. I already felt Italian, but citizenship papers would complete the proof that this was my home.

After a couple of hours of wandering and a *cioccolata calda* at a bar, I hiked down the hill to the train station at San Salvatore, a station I would come to know very well nine years later. I caught a train to Lucca, and from there continued to the coast and then to Cecina. I checked in at Hotel Stella Marina, one of many hotels located right next to the beach. I wanted peace and quiet to write a children's book, and I got all I needed. Cecina was chock full of restaurants and hotels, but almost all were closed in February. Obviously, this town thrived on summer tourism.

After two days, I had finished the book and now wanted a little more noise and action. I called Lucy and we made a plan to meet in a couple of days, and I took a train to Siena. There I rented a car and drove on an unpaved and rocky road through a wilderness reserve near Brenna. After that, I cruised through isolated and scenic mountain roads in southern Toscana, finally ending up in Arezzo, where Lucy joined me for the last three days. Now she would taste freedom from the responsibilities of home for the first time in more than two decades as well. The most memorable place we visited was the Necropolis of Sovana, one of the most impressive remnants of the Etruscan era I have ever seen. These huge and varied tombs, carved out of solid rock, were crafted by the mysterious Etruscans between the seventh and first centuries BC.

The Etruscans were a warlike yet fun-loving people who dominated central Italy long before the Roman Empire came to power. Many of their reliefs and paintings depict them drinking wine and having family parties, a tradition that would later permeate Italian culture into modern times. Their influence on Roman society has only come to be appreciated in the last century. The Etruscans drained marshes, built underground sewers and created roads and bridges using arches. They promoted trade, the development of metallurgy and improved agricultural practices in and around Rome. They introduced the Greek alphabet, and, so respected was their knowledge, the Roman nobles would send their sons to be educated in Etruscan schools. Christian images of demons are said to be modeled after Etruscan demons.

The Romans owed a great deal to the Etruscans. We read that the genius the Romans showed for urban planning, road and bridge building and civil engineering projects such as public aqueducts and baths was a direct result of the legacy left by the Etruscans. The first Roman rulers were Etruscans, and eventually, Etruscan society was peacefully absorbed into Roman society.

Where these people came from has been a mystery for more than two millennia, but I'm inclined to believe Herodotus, who wrote around 450 BC that they came from Lydia in Asia Minor, an area now occupied by Turkey. Recent DNA evidence supports this claim, although some scholars remain unconvinced. Etruscan ruins are scattered throughout central Italy. The name Tuscany is derived from these people, and since my grandparents come from the heart of where their civilization was located, the odds are that I carry a few drops of Etruscan blood, adding to my interest and fascination.

Chapter 18: Becoming more Italian

With white week behind us, we settled back into our school routines. Lucy decided to take a break from Bertrand Russell in March. Though the tuition fees were reasonable and the teachers friendly, Lucy found the curriculum too grammar-oriented. With lessons lasting four hours, the teachers packed so many rules and irregular verbs into one day that students had no time to master one verb tense before the next was introduced. Thus nearly everyone would fail the end-of-course examination and have to repeat the same level. Lindsey also felt frustrated and wanted a change of scenery, so we arranged for her to take a two-week course in language and fashion in Firenze and stay with Silvia and her family. We also found an artist in Padova to meet with Suzye regularly to tutor her in drawing.

Also in March, I caught a bad case of influenza and had to figure out how to maneuver through an Italian hospital to get treated. I had no real health insurance plan because my American insurance would have been too costly to maintain on my meager salary in Italy. Gino had promised he would provide health insurance for my family, but he hadn't realized just how expensive regular insurance would be. After checking into the costs, he asked me to buy travelers insurance, and then he reimbursed me for the fee. The insurance had a high deductible, so that we would be covered for serious illnesses or injuries—but not for influenza.

A few months earlier, Suzye had come down with a throat infection. We couldn't buy any medication because anything strong enough to help would require a visit to the doctor and a prescription. I explained our problem to Gino, and the next day his wife slipped us a bottle of amoxicillin. We didn't ask how she'd arranged that.

The flu really wiped me out, and I knew some antiviral medicine would help me recover more quickly. I could have asked Gino to help again, but my illness was more serious than Suzye's infection had been and would involve a trip to the doctor. I didn't want to take up too much of Gino's time. My Italian was improving, and I figured that some of the hospital personnel would speak English.

As a foreigner, I didn't know if I would be required to pay, but that wasn't my foremost concern. I just wanted to get rid of the fever and ache and get back to work. I made it through the first round of inquiries and form-filling, and within an hour I was given directions to a waiting room, which is where my language skills failed me. After nearly two hours of waiting, I realized that the original dozen patients waiting with me had all been called, and the others around me had all come after me. I checked with the receptionist and she didn't have me on the list, so she got on the phone and determined that I had gone to the wrong waiting room. So much for my improving language skills! I was escorted down a long corridor to the right place and was seen almost immediately. My diagnosis was the flu, and I was given a prescription to fill at the *farmacia* across from the hospital, with no charge for the diagnosis.

I did pay for the medicine, though, and when I got home and took the prescription out of the bag, another cultural difference slowly dawned on me. My medicine was not to be taken orally but rather injected into my posterior. Of course I previously had received vaccinations this way from my doctor, but I had also learned to focus my concentration elsewhere so I could receive the needle without noticing the pain. Actually sticking myself with a needle in the butt seemed an entirely different matter; how could I focus on something else while taking care to put the needle in far enough and then squeezing in the medicine? Suddenly I had a new respect for the courage of the Italian people, who apparently received their prescriptions this way routinely.

Lucy somehow knew this was going to happen. She had read something somewhere in one of the tourist books that Italians are inclined to use this method of medication, but I must have skipped that chapter.

"You could have insisted on oral medicine and they would have given it to you," she said. "You could probably go back to the pharmacy and get a new prescription filled."

Well, too late for that now. I would probably have to pay again for the new prescription, and the cheapskate in me didn't like that idea. My parents had been raised during the depression, and their frugal ways had rubbed off on me. Besides, how could I go up the pharmacist and tell her I didn't have the courage to inject myself? What kind of aspiring Italian citizen says that? If I was going to live like an Italian, I would have to buck up and . . . ask Lucy to give me the injections.

She didn't like that idea at all, but fortunately, she loved me so much that she did it without complaining. I gave her lots of encouragement and brave talk about how it wouldn't hurt me at all, and I always kept talking away and managed to avoid flinching when she did the deed so she wouldn't feel traumatized. I'm sure if I had screamed like a hyena, she would have been too shell-shocked to continue the series of injections day after day, which she faithfully did, bless her loving soul. Thankfully, the medicine worked very efficiently, and my flu retreated rapidly.

The only glitch came when I returned to school, and Lucy came to give me the last scheduled injection. She was loading the syringe in my empty classroom when in walked Bruna, the Italian teacher, to pick up some papers she had left behind. Lucy tried to explain in English that she was not some stray drug addict who had found an empty room in which to shoot up. She was met only with a suspicious gaze, because Bruna didn't understand English, but I walked in a moment later, and together we were able to clarify the situation to Bruna's satisfaction. The only problem is that Lucy was laughing so much after Bruna left that she could hardly hold the needle steady.

With the last dose finally injected, I can say that I can't believe those wimpy Americans who only take their medicines orally, not like us stoic and fearless Italians who laugh at the thought of pain.

That evening, Lucy and I celebrated my recovery by taking a stroll in Piazza Garibaldi. It was warm enough that a restaurant had set up tables outside in the piazza. As we paused to consider sitting down, a waiter showed us an appealing menu and told us there was no *coperto*, cover charge. We were trying to conserve our money and eat meals in our apartment, but it was such a beautiful evening, the girls were out with friends, and we had not yet had our fill of the sights and sounds of the piazza. We succumbed to the waiter's charm and the irresistible odors wafting out of the kitchen.

We each had our personal favorite *primi piatti*: spaghetti alla carbonara for Lucy and pesto genovese for me. We noticed the attention the restaurant paid to style and detail, something that we often observed when doing business with Italians. We were given a colorful basket with three types of bread, artfully arranged. Our table service was wrapped in a paper envelope imprinted with flowers. The waiter, in his mid-twenties, had already mastered that easy-going Italian charm and attentiveness that embody *la bella figura*. He immediately brought to mind the courtly mannerisms cited by the fifteenth century count Baldassarre Castiglione, who served in several royal courts. In his book *Il Libro del Cortegiano*—The Book of the Courtesan—Castiglione gave advice on how to be a gentleman. He even invented a word to describe his ideal, *sprezzatura*, which means the studied carelessness that conceals art and presents everything said and done as something brought about without laboriousness and almost without giving it any thought. Author Dianna Hales has explained that the "closest English translation is 'nonchalance,' which fails to capture the behind-the-scenes preparation and hard work that underlies the ability to carry off 'things that are exquisite and well done'—be it a duel, debate or dance, executed with such ease that it inspires 'the greatest wonder.' This is the essence of *bella figura*."

As I gave my credit card to pay the *conto*, I found that our waiter's courtly behavior likely came from the fine family line of his mother. He noticed my name on the card. "Spadoni!" he said. "*Mia madre si chiama Spadoni.*" His mother was a

Spadoni from Rome, so the confluence of our families could be 1,000 years distant, if at all. Still, it was nice to have this added connection as a fitting conclusion to our elegant little lunch break.

Chapter 19: Conflicts at home

One day while tidying up the house, my curiosity about my daughters' safety during their late-night excursions with their Italian school friends overcame me. I did something I had never done before. I looked in Suzye's journal to find out what went on in their nights in the dance clubs. I didn't make this decision lightly. I know it's a struggle that many parents face, and I based it on the fact that my daughters were at risk of making foolish choices that might adversely affect their futures. My own parents had been fairly permissive with me, and I had done some incredibly stupid things that could have had severe consequences if something had gone wrong.

The first few incidents I read gave me no cause for concern. They had taken the train to a dance club in Bologna after telling us they would be in Padova. Mild stuff, and besides, after that incident they had asked if they could go to some other cities and we had given permission. On another occasion, a girl named Silvia had been driving, with her boyfriend in the front seat and Suzye, Lindsey and Erica in the back. Silvia started passionately making out with her boyfriend while driving, and the girls in the back kept yelling at her to pay attention to her driving. Finally, Erica insisted that Silvia pull over and let them out. They walked the rest of the way and found out the next day that Silvia and her *ragazzo* had driven off the road. Silvia and the boy had leaped out of the car before it fell over a bank, and they were unhurt. Any passengers in the backseat of this two-door car would not have been able to get out so easily, so it had been a close call. Ultimately, though this qualified as risky behavior, I had to admire the wisdom and maturity of Erica for saving herself and my daughters from injury.

I also discovered that Suzye had briefly had a boyfriend, of sorts, one of her classmates named Marco. We had met him briefly, and he seemed like a nice guy, and we knew they had gone on at least one date. They had engaged in some kissing, but the next day at school, Marco had exaggerated the extent of their intimacy to his friends, and Suzye refused to date him again.

I worried a little when I read about a late-night incident in a small town near Padova: "We had to wait two hours for the next train, and there was no place to sit down. The people in the station were not travelers but seemed like they lived there or did some sort of illicit business there. We went to stand next to an old lady, thinking we would be safer, but then we realized something wasn't quite right. She was wearing a LOT of makeup. That's when we realized she was not an old lady at all but a man in heavy makeup." This is not something that makes a dad happy to hear, but still it was not a deal breaker. I felt there was safety in numbers and was glad to read that the girls were paying attention to their surroundings.

That would have been the end of my snooping had it not been for one incriminating entry. In the fall, Suzye and Lindsey had been together in a park, and someone had offered to sell them hashish. They bought it and smoked it together. The entry included no other details, so I assumed nothing else had occurred, but this could not be so easily dismissed, and now I faced an unpleasant dilemma. If I confronted Suzye and

Lindsey with the entry, they would know I had read Suzye's journal. This violation of trust would surely damage our relationship at a time when our relationship was already on shaky ground. I struggled for a few days with the decision. I didn't want to fess up to my snooping, because even though I could justify it in my parental mind as part of my protective duties, I was sure the girls would see it differently.

In the end, I handled it badly. I consulted Lucy, who had been unaware of my actions and didn't approve of them. Of course, she also didn't want her daughters taking drugs, so after giving it a couple more days of thought, she ratted me out for ratting them out. She confronted the girls and told them what I had read. The girls readily accepted their blame, apologized quickly and promised that it wouldn't happen again. This spared me the direct conflict of having to reprimand them for bad behavior that I had discovered through my own questionable ethics. However, I should have been the one to talk to them, so that at least they could confront me with my actions, and we could have had a conversation about what led me to do it. It's a regret that I carry with me still.

Ironically, I learned through an overheard conversation between Lindsey and another friend why the girls had been so ready to repent and ask forgiveness. It seems that Lindsey had read Lucy's diary, which said: "Paul found out by reading Suzye's journal that the girls smoked hashish last fall. He doesn't want them to know he read it, but I think I'm going to talk to them."

Suzye had apparently been at a loss about what to do, but Lindsey had advised: "Let's just confess, say we're sorry and promise not to do it again." I heard Lindsey add to the friend: "It worked perfectly. We weren't punished at all. And Suzye threw away her journal after that."

Why, that little double dealing rascal! Reading someone's private journal? I should give her . . . oh, wait. Never mind. Let's just consider that the score was even and we're starting over again.

Chapter 20: Scope for the imagination

My sister Linda came for a visit in March, about a week before my school's spring break. Because Linda is a retired teacher and born story-teller, I worked out the schedule so that she would be available when it was my turn to lead the elementary school's weekly assembly. This way, I only had to introduce her and let her do the rest, an easy way to fulfill my responsibility.

We took a weekend trip to Montecatini to visit cousins Enrico and Loriano and their families. By then, our Italian had improved enough to allow us to hold rudimentary conversations. During dinner, Enrico asked me an intriguing and impossible-to-answer question: "Aside from our obviously superior food, why do you want to live in Italy?"

It seemed evident from some disparaging comments he had made about Italy earlier as well as his tone of voice and body language that he considered the quality of life in Italy to be heading downhill. He considered America superior in many ways.

I tried to answer, but since my language skills lacked the sophistication to explain fully, most of the following explanation took place only in my mind. I could find the words in English, but not in Italian. However, here is what I tried to say.

"It's not just the better food but also the local markets. I walk through nearly any medium to large Italian city and find a traveling market set up in a piazza. It might be for vegetables and fruit, home wares, clothing, antiques, flowers, CDs and

DVDs, books, artwork—or even live chickens. We like the prices, but even if we're not buying anything, we like seeing a colorful close-up slice of living.

"We also like that we can catch a train or bus to every medium-sized or large city in the country. You can take a bike on the train, and you can get off the train in a city along the way, grab some food or do some exploring, and then hop on the next train to continue to your destination still using the same ticket.

"But probably what I like best is that it gives me scope for the imagination. Leonardo da Vinci said, 'The faculty of imagination is both the rudder and the bridle of the senses.' When I drive through the Italian countryside, I wonder what hardships a city must have experienced during the two world wars, when sons were sent away to bloody battles in icy Russia and German soldiers took over Italian cities and farms. Every city has a monument to the lives lost. What was it like to be in Italy during the late 1800s and early 1900s when millions of people were leaving for new countries? What hardships did our great grandfather Spadoni and his father face as *contadini* during the 1800s? This was at the time when Italy changed from being a conglomeration of city-states to a unified country. And looking back earlier than the *Risorgimento* (Unification), what were the Spadonis and Seghieris doing during the Renaissance? What would it have been like to know Michelangelo or Leonardo or Cosimo de' Medici? Imagine having Galileo as your professor.

"I've only covered a short span of history with these imaginings. Italy has been invaded and/or occupied by Goths, Huns, Lombards, Byzantines, Francs, Arabs, Germans,

Spanish, Austrians, French, popes and more. Earlier, of course, were the Romans, and before that the Greeks, and then there were those mysterious Etruscans. And who lived here before that?"

"Beh," Enrico answered. "It was all well enough for you and Leonardo to have imagination. But Leonardo didn't have to spend half his earnings on taxes like we do and deal with dozens of political parties and overpaid politicians. Or spend thousands of lira just to get *permesso* to build a pizza oven in his own backyard."

Chapter 21: Cultural observations

Another inconvenience Leonardo da Vinci avoided was that famous Italian event, *Lo Sciopero*. An Italian strike is vastly different than one in America. *Scioperi* usually last no more than a day, sometimes only a few hours. Often affecting the transit industry, they are almost invariably announced long in advance, and there are web sites where one can find out who will be on strike when and make alternate plans. The grandaddy of all strikes is the national strike (*sciopero generale*), a day on which all public transportation may be stopped or at least restricted. Garbage won't be collected, museums and governmental office will be closed, and even some private businesses like grocery stores close in sympathy. Usually nobody knows the reason for any particular strike, other than that "it must be about working conditions"—but it could just be an excuse for another day off. We had a few spring days when the bus drivers were on strike, but the weather had turned warm by March, and I was often riding my bike to school by then.

Italians learn the art of the sciopero early. Suzye's fellow students at Gramsci participated in periodic strikes throughout the year. Suzye said none of her friends offered any specific reasons for the strikes, but they sometimes participated, which simply meant that they didn't go to school and instead hung out with each other in the city center. While most student strikes also involved a *manifestazione*—a demonstration—only a handful of striking students attended the demonstration.

Luca Mammi, the son of Stefano and Nancy, provided us with better insight on these events.

"In a poorly organized strike," he said, "maybe only one or two people will go to the demonstration. But for a major strike, one that we felt was important, as many as 90 percent of my class will miss school, and about half will go the demonstration. The school has to stay open by law, but when most students are missing, nothing happens in the class."

Do strikes have any effects? Obviously, this is open to interpretation, but Luca didn't think the student strikes helped at all.

"I've only taken part in one strike," he said. "It was one of the poorly organized ones, with no more that forty people and a pickup truck with music and a guy shouting slogans. It felt like a traveling party, and I couldn't shake the feeling that most of the people were there to stay out of school."

Fortunately, no strikes were held during our spring break. Suzye and Lindsey traveled to England for Suzye's class trip, a tradition for the Gramsci graduating class. Even though Lindsey had dropped out months before and had been in a different class, the school graciously allowed her to be part of the group. Suzye and Lindsey left for London in late March. For my spring vacation, Gino had given me permission to extend it for three additional days, so Linda, Lucy and I headed by train to Napoli, a memorable city in many ways.

The traffic amazed us, as there seemed to be no rules, but the more I studied it, the more I realized how wrong I was. The rules existed and everyone knew them well; they were just different from my expectations. We spent about twenty minutes on a bridge in Napoli, watching the busy and scary streets down below. We observed how amazingly smoothly the traffic flowed. If two cars were approaching the same intersection at the same time at a ninety degree angle, it looked like a collision would occur because neither car was slowing down. However, as they got closer, it became apparent that one car was about five feet closer to the intersection than the other. The car that was behind braked just the slightest bit, allowing the other driver to enter the intersection first, but then the second car continued at almost the same speed and zipped just a few feet behind the first car. It looked like a narrow miss, but both drivers understood the rules, and the traffic flow continued with only an imperceptible interruption. In America, both cars would have slowed way down, and then one driver would signal the other to go ahead, in a very safe and logical way, it would seem. However, the Italian drivers caused much less disruption to the flow of traffic, and since the roads were crowded, traffic would have been at a perpetual standstill under American rules.

We also learned two valuable lessons from old ladies. Once we were trying to cross a busy city arterial during rush hour in a place where there was no intersection to slow down the traffic. Cars were speeding by continuously, and we waited for several minutes for a break, with no success. Up marched an ancient lady in a black dress and carrying a bag of groceries. She held up her hand, palm out, and stepped boldly out into the traffic and crossed the street. Cars careened to a stop—or at least slowed down enough so they didn't hit her. We were so entranced by the scene that we missed our chance to cross with her, but we employed the same technique a minute later, and it worked just fine.

Napoli is known to have a higher crime rate than the rest of Italy, and I noticed that nearly half of the parked cars had steering wheel locks, something I had rarely seen in Padova. As we came up the stairs from the train, a dignified looking lady going down stopped Linda, and using a few words and lots of gestures, indicated that Linda must carry her purse with the strap over her head, not just over her shoulder, and with both arms across it. I thought this piece of kindness said a lot about Napoli. On the one hand, it is full of thieves who might snatch a purse. On the other hand, it is full of helpful, kindly people who will go out of their way to advise a total stranger.

We went to the Museo Archeologico Nazionale, which has a fantastic collection of Greek and Roman antiquities, many of which came from the nearby excavations at Pompeii and Herculaneum, well-preserved sites that were buried by the eruption of Mount Vesuvius in 79 AD. The display of mosaics and frescoes was impressive, and it was especially helpful to see a three-dimensional display of the excavations at Pompeii to help orient us for the next day. The exhibit of erotic art from Pompeii is well worth seeing; it is really more funny than it is erotic, and it shows you that boastfulness over male anatomical size is certainly not a recent development. I would bet that someone selling a size-enhancing cream or elixir in Pompeii would have made a fortune, although it would have been advisable to leave town before 79 AD rolled around.

The next day we took the train to see Pompeii close up, and it is still one of our most memorable Italian experiences. I always like to imagine what the world was like in the past, and Pompeii provides a clear window into the everyday life of

2,000 years ago. As we walked the streets of this once bustling town, we looked into the houses, shops, bars and bathhouses that were so well preserved by a sudden act of God. It was a very different life and also very much the same. You can also quite literally see the shapes of the last inhabitants as they passed away.

A stray dog adopted us for a while, and we nicknamed him Guido because he seemed to be acting like our own personal *guida*, or guide. At a certain spot, he would go no further, and we realized there are many strays in old Pompeii, and each has its territory. Guido knew how far he could go without encroaching on his neighbor's land.

We overheard a tour guide explaining to his group that dogs were an important part of society in Pompeii, used both as pets and to guard people's homes, as they are now. In fact, we saw the first known "beware of the dog" sign in the House of the Tragic Poet in Pompeii—a mosaic with a barking dog chained up. Below is the warning in Latin: *Cave Canem.*

"Dogs were protected by law from ill-treatment, as dogs are now," the guide said. "Those dogs who were unchained, sensing the geological unrest, probably fled the city in advance of the eruption. Those who were chained perished along with their owners." Indeed, we saw a plaster cast display of a dog, wearing a bronze-studded collar, which had perished while chained up on guard duty.

"The dogs who live here now are strays," the guide continued. "They are still on guard, but now it's for handouts of a bite to eat—yet they all have a special dignity. They are still protected. We guides care for them by pooling money to pay for food."

That night, we slept in the center of Pompeii—not the city that had been buried but the one that had been rebuilt after the eruption. When we went for a stroll in the *centro* around 9 p.m., we were amazed to see the street and squares packed with locals strolling around and going no place in particular. It was the famous Italian *passeggiata*, something we not yet experienced in Padova because we lived in the suburbs and didn't go to the *centro* at night, although we later discovered that Padova and every Italian city of decent size has an evening *passeggiata*. It is a wonder to behold and among Italy's most poignant traditions.

I struggle with words to describe *la passeggiata*. It is a slow and gentle stroll through the pedestrian parts of the center of any city, usually beginning just before dusk. It signals the end of the work day, offers a breath of fresh air and allows people to chat with friends and neighbors. On weekends whole families walk together, sometimes splitting apart for smaller conversations and then joining together again.

"This is astounding," Lucy said. "How did we miss this up to now? It's like an all-inclusive, multi-generational town party. People greet their friends and neighbors, swap gossip, share the latest news. It reminds me of a blanket, where every thread is a person, woven together into one human fabric."

And speaking of fabric, these Italians knew how to dress up. Lucy and I are not into clothing and fashion by any stretch of the imagination. Lucy has to practically drag me along when I need to go shopping for clothes, and I rely on her judgment more than my own, but even she admits to being clueless compared to the average Italian. However, even the most fashion-challenged person in the world can't help but appreciate the daily fashion shows that take place on the city sidewalks. People here like to look good, and even as we walk around in our blue jeans and sweatshirts, we can't help but appreciate these well-dressed and coiffed *italiani*.

I could say that people dress carefully for this special stroll, but the fact is that most Italians almost always look good in public. Clothes are stylish but not garish. Colors are coordinated; styles are modern, classy and form-fitting, never faded or sagging. Sweatpants and sweatshirts are virtually non-existent. Yet these people dress in a way that looks natural, effortless. It is another example of *sprezzatura*.

Sprezzatura in clothing, according to fashionista Johnny Liu, is "artful dishevelment—dressing like you don't care, taking a nonchalant attitude with your appearance—when in fact you do take time and effort to create your look. The trick to pulling it off is subtlety, confidence and an otherwise impeccable outfit."

"I'll never be that Italian," I told Lucy. "Are they just born knowing how to dress and look sharp and beautiful? I'm missing that gene."

"No, it's obvious that they've learned it while growing up," she said. "I'm sure they pay plenty of attention to the way they look and dress—but we're from Washington. We've made the grunge look famous."

But a passeggiata goes far beyond simple fashions. Old people are out and about, walking slowly, faces lined with character and experience. I can imagine that the old man I see might have been, one hundred years earlier, my own great grandfather, walking along with hands behind his back, or playing checkers with another old timer on a park bench. The old woman could have been my great grandmother, and the middle-aged woman walking with her, arms linked, my grandmother. I instantly sense that something is fundamentally different about these people, and as I sit and watch carefully, I notice the way they interact. Many people walk with their arms linked together. Of course this applies to couples of all ages and is not unique to Italy. But it is also common to see teenage girls with linked arms, a sign of close friendship, and teen girls linked to their mothers. Middle-aged women walk with arms linked to their aging mothers. Sometimes sisters walk on either side of a particularly old mother to offer both physical and emotional support.

This closeness is not limited to the women. While it is unusual to see boys walking with linked arms, there still is a physical closeness and comfort with contact not seen in other countries. I see a cluster of boys talking loudly and easily with each other, and one puts his hand on the other's shoulder and leans closer to share a story he does not want everyone else to hear. It is also possible to see middle-aged men with arms linked to their fathers, and even occasionally a young teen boy linked with father or mother, something that would be social suicide in America. The closeness of Italian family ties is typically something that people note and admire about Italy, and the *passeggiata* develops and encourages this trait as well as puts it on display.

While most people walk in groups, those walking by themselves seem perfectly comfortable among the crowd. At a certain age—maybe the mid-sixties—men walking by themselves adopt what Lucy and I call "old man walk," leaning forward slightly, with hands clasped behind their backs. Body language specialists suggest this posture demonstrates a self-confident person who has lived a satisfied and fulfilled life. I occasionally practice this myself when walking alone so I will be ready when my time comes.

Watching the teenagers interact during the evening passeggiata is another fascinating experience. Groups meet, mix and split into different groups. Rarely is anyone walking alone, and if they are, they are probably on a cell phone, planning a rendezvous. Teenagers and young adults perhaps have the most at stake when it comes to making *la bella figura*. This is their chance to strengthen friendships, make new ones and impress the opposite sex. In a way, the passeggiata of young people reminds me of middle and high school dances, charged with youthful energy, enthusiasm and passion, a socially sanctioned opportunity for flirting and courtship. Parents approve because the interpersonal skills gained are useful in the workplace and the complex politics of life. Of course this event takes place every night, so the stakes are not so high and the participants more relaxed, experienced and comfortable.

"Look at those men sitting together around that table," Lucy said. "You should go join them. You look Italian. You'd probably fit right in."

"Yeah, I wish," I replied. "Other than the fact that I wouldn't understand a word they were saying, and vice-versa. Besides, even if I could understand their Italian—which is probably mostly dialect—I don't do well in groups even when the men are speaking English. But I do envy them. If I had been raised here, maybe I would have developed better social skills as a youth, and then I could be comfortable sitting around chatting, arguing, playing cards with my lifelong friends."

"Or at least by now you would have mastered the old man walk," Lucy said.

We continued to visit more typical tourist sites: Capri, Pisa, Cinque Terre, Firenze and Fiesole. Once, while waiting for a train in Napoli, we encountered an enterprising hustler who offered his services to help us find the right train and carry our luggage, though we needed help with neither.

"I work for the train company," he lied, pointing to the Trenitalia logo on a faded and slightly tattered shirt that he had likely bought at a second-hand store. "I'm here to help you find your train. Where are you going?"

He caught me off guard, and I gave him my destination without thinking. Then we had to put up with his "help" while we waited fifteen minutes for our train.

"You need to stand right over here," he said, picking up Lucy's suitcase and moving it about ten feet from where we were already standing. "Don't worry, I'll get you on the right train." Then he pounced on an elderly British couple who were scrutinizing their tickets. Now he had five people to herd, and he kept trying to move us to less crowded parts of the platform, fussing like a mother hen and constantly assuring us we were in the right spot and our train would come soon. Where had this guy been when I was trying to handle three large suitcases and a carry-on in September?

We realized that he was doing all this so we would tip him at the end, and of course he insisted on carrying suitcases for Lucy and the British lady onto the train. He held out his hand,

and I gave him a meager tip. He looked sadly at the single coin in his hand, his face imploring me for more generosity. My inherited frugality won out. I shook my head, indicating this was all he would get. We had not asked for his help. I did feel a little bad, because at least he was providing a service instead of begging for a handout, and some new travelers probably found his kind of help useful.

On a crowded bus up the hill to Fiesole, Linda was mistaken for an Italian by some elderly British ladies. She overheard them fussing about how the bus was so crowded that they couldn't get to the front to put their tickets in the validation machine. They were worried about getting a fine, which was pretty ridiculous, considering how rarely the bus police actually checked for tickets and also how impossible it was for everyone to reach the machine. Linda tried to tell them, in English, not to worry about it, but before she could even start, they held up their hands, "No, no, no! We don't speak Italian. Only English." Amused, Linda paused a moment and looked thoughtful, and then she tried again, holding up her own ticket and saying slowly and with an exaggerated Italian accent: "Eez permeeta to do teeketa at stazi . . . station." The English ladies were thrilled and grateful that the little Italian lady had been so kind to use her limited English to help them. In truth, there is no ticket validation machine for buses at the station, but the English ladies wouldn't listen to the truth. Now they were happy, and Linda was pleased that she had found a clever way to make them stop fussing— although glad that she'd be getting off the bus before the station.

Chapter 22: Making progress

"The mind can be compared to a plant," I read in a health advice website. "If you 'water' it through mental activity and challenges, it will grow. Although a brain may get old, it still produces new cells that aid in communications between different parts of the brain and in the retrieval of information."

I hope this is true, I told myself, because my mind was certainly getting a great workout. Sometimes I questioned whether my brain might be an exception. Had it stopped producing new cells, because I was learning so slowly? It was particularly frustrating because I could speak and write English so easily, and you'd think that would have helped me learn Italian more quickly, but there is no magic ticket. I struggled along slowly, not being able to tell from week to week if I was really improving. Nonetheless, it was a challenge that overall I enjoyed facing, and though I had a long way to go, at times I recognized that I had come a long way as well.

In early April, we found an important use for our slowly improving Italian. Around 11 p.m., a rap on our door jolted us awake. It was Cristina from next door, and she was worried about her mom. Signora Maggiore was weak and vomiting, so I called the emergency medical phone number and explained the situation. An ambulance came and took her away, and we found out the next day she had suffered a mild heart attack and would be hospitalized for a week. That night Lucy stayed overnight with Cristina, but she seemed okay staying by herself after that, and we checked in on her occasionally.

Because Cristina had never lived alone, Signora Maggiore had often expressed her concern about what Cristina would do when the Signora's health failed. Signora Maggiore came back in a week and didn't have any further health problems that year. We felt pleased that we had been able to help in a small way.

Suzye quit her Italian school after the class trip to England so she could focus on finishing her correspondence and online courses. Through a combination of procrastination and our busy schedules, both she and Lindsey had fallen far behind, and they spent a lot of time at my school in April and May. Eventually, they did catch up, and they completed their courses successfully with a few days to spare. They still went out often with Erica and their other Italian friends, and by this time they were no longer complaining about being in Italy.

"Are they actually happy now?" I asked Lucy one evening.

"I think they just might be," she replied with a look of surprise. "I haven't given it much thought recently, but it's been a long time since anyone cried or asked to go home."

We agreed that we wouldn't try to drag confessions out of them that their parents might have been right all along. We didn't want to come across as sanctimonious, but we definitely noted signs of maturity, responsibility and stability. We didn't to press our good fortune too far. We would wait to see what they might say in a few more months.

Meanwhile, my fifth-grade class was anticipating the highlight of the academic year—sex education! I had to admit that this was a good age to study the topic. We had been studying the human body all year: eyes, ears, tongue, digestion, heart and other important organs. My students always peppered me with interesting questions. Now it was time to study the last of those important organs, and the questions came as usual, with no signs of any embarrassment. I think I had developed the right balance between connectedness and separation with my students to explain the details of sex and sexuality easily. We had developed strong bonds during the year, but I was still a respected authority figure—not a familiar one like a parent, but more like a medical doctor. Frankly, I did a lot better teaching these ten- and eleven-year-old *ragazzi* than I had done with my kids.

Catherine, on the other hand, looked on the required sex lessons with dread. She was only about fifteen years older than her students, and she was recently engaged to be married. Perhaps she worried that the question and answer sessions might become too personal. Since she had taught music to my students during the year, I volunteered to teach the sex unit to her class. They had fewer questions than my class, probably because they didn't know me as well, but all in all, it went amazingly well. Many people have told me that Italians are more comfortable discussing sex without embarrassment than are Americans, and this could be a reason for the matter-of-fact way the students received and discussed the facts of life, but maybe all fifth graders are like this.

I did have one touchy discussion at recess with a student I will call Giancarlo. He was red-faced and angry with some of his friends, and it looked like he was about to lose his temper, so I separated them. Then I asked Giancarlo what was going on. At first, he didn't want to tell me, but I pressed him a little harder.

"Pōl-uh, you know the thing of the man," he said, *sotto voce* and casting his eyes downward. I nodded.

"Well, they said that I put mine inside Gina, but I didn't."

I rolled my eyes. "Giancarlo, why do you think they said this?"

He thought about this. "To make me angry."

"And what do you think would happen if you didn't get angry?"

"Maybe they would stop saying it."

"I think so too. Let's try that next time and see how it works." Apparently, it did.

One of the side benefits of teaching so many subjects was that it gave me an opportunity to study Italian history as part of the curriculum. We covered the years of the French Revolution through World War II, all from a European perspective. In order to prepare and augment the lessons, I studied other sources, and so I learned much more than the class did. As we studied World War I, I was struck by all the alliances the nations had formed before the war. Country A agreed that it would defend Country B in the event of war. B would side with C, C with D and D with E. Thus when E went to war with F, all the others were committed as well. Of course F also had its chain of alliances, so nearly all of Europe and scattered other parts of the world were almost immediately drawn into full-fledged conflict. However, there was always the chance that a country would refuse to honor its pre-war agreement or even change loyalties.

This reminded me so much of the board game called Risk that I wanted my students to play the game so they could feel the moral conflict involved in being compelled to honor an old alliance made in all sincerity but which no longer served their own interests. I've heard stories of players who had destroyed long-standing friendships over broken Risk alliances or feelings of being persecuted by the other players. However, knowing that the game can last all day, I couldn't justify using that much class time, so I could only explain the general rules and recommend that they play the game at home. I knew that there is an Italian version called Risiko, though the rules are slightly different. My desire to introduce them to Risk sparked my thinking, and I came up with an idea that turned out to be the highlight of the school year, a memorable experience for us all.

I designed a plan to combine a game of Risk with two other group experiences: a cram-session for the school exams, and an end-of-the-year overnight celebration. The inspiration for the event came from my twenty-one years as a high school newspaper adviser, when our final session to put an issue of the newspaper together lasted from after school Friday until late in the evening and often even all night—with lots of breaks for talking, eating and excursions to the store to get more goodies in between the actual work sessions.

I proposed—first to Gino and Angela—that my class be allowed to have an extended after-school study session, which would then morph into an overnight party, with a game of Risk included as a transition from the actual study time to the fun and games time. Guys would sleep with me in Catherine's classroom and girls with Lucy in my room. I thought that Gino or Angela might veto the plan out of concerns for liability or safety, but they thought it was a great idea. The kids were highly enthused when I shared the idea with them. Naturally the word they singled out most quickly in my explanation was "party," but I stressed that the purpose was to prepare for the exams while having a *little* fun. I continued to emphasize this aspect in the week before the event, but I was well prepared to devote a substantial amount of the event to fun. They had worked hard during the year and in truth were prepared for the exams without extra study. The purpose of the special session was to make them feel more confident by having extra preparation, to reward them for being such a great group—and to play Risk.

We focused on study time in the afternoon and ended the work portion with a shortened version of Risk. They were not as patient during the game as I had hoped, but they did last long enough to experience the conflicts of making and breaking alliances. Parent volunteers provided us with dinner, and we watched part of the movie *Pearl Harbor* to go along with our study of World War II. Then we played "sardines," a variant of hide and seek, where one child hid in the dark on the upper floor of the elementary school. Everyone else was a seeker. When a seeker found the hider by feeling around in near blackness, the seeker had to join by hiding in the same place—while trying to resist giggling or making any other sounds. After a while, only one seeker would remain, although by the end, it was not difficult to locate thirteen other fifth graders all packed together in one place, trying without success to be perfectly quiet.

I had some momentary apprehension when one of the girls screamed out, "He touched my boobies! He touched my boobies!" Was some unfortunate sexual advance going to spoil our evening? But it turned out that the seeking boy merely had his hands extended in the dark while trying to find a small group of hiders. In the darkness, he made contact entirely by accident. I spoke to the girl and she seemed to understand the circumstances completely, but a minute later she yelled out one more time, "He touched my boobies." I think she may have been enjoying the extra attention just a little. The boy had already apologized and the event didn't become an issue.

With the study party behind us, the school exams passed quickly and uneventfully. Examiners pulled students out of the classroom one at a time, and upon returning, each student said how easy it had been. Some were even disappointed that they weren't given a chance to fully demonstrate the vast knowledge they had gained during the year.

With exam pressure a thing of the past, a new oppression came from the heat. Once June hit, I realized why Italians living inland all try to go to the beach or the mountains in the summer. We opened wide every window and door, but by midday, I found myself dripping with perspiration. One day we received permission to go to the park with Catherine's class, and the last day Lucy and I took my class to a *gelateria*, a sweet ending to a very pleasant nine months.

Chapter 23: Making ends meet

As the school year wound down and the heat cranked up, it was time to say good-bye to my colleagues and supervisors. As it turned out, I had developed a strong rapport with the students and pushed them plenty hard enough to please Gino and the parents, so no one dropped out of my class.

All my encounters with Gino had been positive experiences, but I also knew he had a reputation as a clever businessman. One of the other teachers once told me, "Gino cares only about three things: money, money and money." In some ways, this did seem true. For example, according to the nursery school teachers, he allowed children under the minimum age to enroll in the nursery. He accepted students in the middle grades who spoke no English in order to increase his enrollment, making it very difficult for the teachers to cope because of the extra attention these students needed. I experienced his financial acumen first-hand when I went to receive my final pay in June. I had made some discreet inquiries and discovered that indeed my monthly pay was slightly higher than that of my colleagues, as Gino had pledged. However, we had never discussed whether this included only the ten months school was in session or was an annual contract, which is normal in education. I should have inquired about this when I was hired, but it didn't cross my mind until later. In my twenty years of teaching in the states, I had always had my pay divided over twelve months, but how did it work at Gino's school? I didn't know, but I would soon find out. I walked into his office on the last day of school to collect my cash payment. Gino paid me only for June and thanked me for my year of service. This led to an awkward discussion in which I admitted that I hadn't asked before if I was getting paid for twelve months, but I knew that was customary in both Italy and the United States. He suggested that he could pay me for an extra month, and not wanting to push my point, I agreed.

I had a discussion with Angela and I found out what a bargain I had been to Gino, even with the additional month of pay. All the British teachers worked on a contract negotiated by a British agency and were paid year-round. Not only that, but there is also a custom in Italy called the thirteenth month, in which workers receive an extra month of pay at the end of the year. The British teachers would be paid for thirteen months, Angela said. So though I received a bigger paycheck for eleven months, I would still get less than all the other teachers. Although Angela was really part of management, she didn't think I was getting a fair deal and suggested I talk to Gino again.

When I explained what I knew about the thirteen-month contracts the other teachers had, Gino squirmed a bit and asked what I was proposing. I told him I would be happy with another half month of pay, which would bring my salary close to that of the other teachers. I really had no bargaining power, as we had no written contract, but happily, he agreed. Well, I looked happy; he didn't. Still, Gino ended the year saving money by hiring me, and if even one disgruntled set of parents had pulled their child out of school, Gino would have lost much more money than he spent to keep me happy. Truth be told, I still felt fortunate that I had been able to find a job for one year and have all my housing needs supplied. So despite Gino's initial ploy, I still left the school with positive feelings and, temporarily, a pocketful of cash.

Overall, our money situation did not end positively, however. We had paid for private language lessons and had taken extensive trips during winter break, white week and spring break, and before we returned in early July, we traveled for another two weeks to the island of Ischia and then the Ligurian coast, just to enjoy the beaches and be typical tourists. We even made a one-day foray in France. With these trips, along with our moving expenses, we ended up at least $20,000 in debt when we arrived home. Even so, I had no regrets whatsoever.

Chapter 24: An end that is actually a beginning

As our time in Padova drew to a close, Lucy and I spent some time discussing our successes and failures. I had found a rewarding job and a great place to live in the fascinating ancient city of Padova. Lucy had learned to shop like an Italian, buying fresh artisan goods at a variety of small Italian stores instead of stocking up on prepared goods for a week at a supermarket. She blended her American and Italian cooking skills ably, and our entire family's palette and diet improved dramatically over the course of the year. We could travel around Italy with ease and communicate on a basic level. Our family had drawn closer together, and the girls were no longer complaining about living in Italy. In these situations, we had managed to live our bold dream with great success.

"So, are you happy with the way things have worked out?" Lucy asked as we were packing. "You've lived your dream, and we've all—even Suzye and Lindsey—had an incredible time."

"Yes, of course," I said. "At times I can hardly believe how blessed we've been. It makes me laugh when I think that I had planned to find both a job and an apartment by coming here only ten days before you guys."

Still, I felt something lacking, as if Italy and I had unfinished business to transact. Two of my main goals—to learn Italian and understand what it was like to live an Italian lifestyle—were not going to be fully realized. I had spoken English all day at school and English at home. I had written lesson plans in English. At church, most people spoke English as a common language. Our best friends, the Grays and Mammis, spoke English with us. I was coming to the conclusion that as interesting as this year was turning out, it wasn't going to get the bug for Italian culture out of my system.

Teaching new subject matter at an unfamiliar grade level meant I had taken a lot of time preparing lessons as well as teaching and grading work. Lucy had taken four sessions of language lessons and made friends with her classmates from other countries, but with the exception of Stefano Mammi, neither of us had made any close Italian friends, and we were still miles away from being conversant in Italian.

We had accumulated four used bikes, some furniture and lots of kitchen utensils from a nearby second-hand store, and we had purchased new ceramic tableware. We had originally thought that we would donate most of these things to the church. Steve and Patti could distribute them to needy newcomers to the community.

"We have plenty of room in our basement," Patti said. "You don't need to give away everything. We'll just keep it here until you move back to Italy."

She said this half jokingly, but also with a ray of hopefulness. We had become good friends, and they would dearly miss us, she added.

Could we somehow find a way to come back to Italy? For the first time, I began to think about retiring from teaching so that I could really enjoy myself and gain a more thorough understanding of Italian living. We had come to Italy in large part to explore the culture and experience life the way Italians did, and on this score, we had failed. We still felt very separate from the natives. We found Italians friendly and gracious, but because we were foreigners, we operated in different spheres. We felt very much at home with the Grays and Mammis, but we quickly ran out of words on the rare occasions we were with Italian couples for any extended time.

"You know what?" I told Lucy. "We're not done here."

"I know," she said. "We still have to pack our things from the bathroom."

"No, that's not what I mean. I'm saying we're not done with Italy. We have to find a way to come back and do this again. But do it even better."

We would have to return, but not to work, because it took up too much of my time, and especially not in an English-speaking environment. We needed to live in a city where few people spoke English, so we would be forced to speak Italian and have Italians as friends. Too often when we went into a store or hotel and asked for something in Italian, we would be answered in English. Our accents, our style of dress, Lucy's blond hair all gave us away, and the clerks in tourist cities usually wanted to practice their English or make us feel more at home by responding with familiar words.

How I could swing that I didn't know, because I was only 49, far from retirement age. To receive full state retirement benefits, I would have to teach until I was 64. Still, I didn't want to give up hope, and the Grays encouraged us and insisted they had plenty of storage space, even if we didn't come back for fifteen years. So we packed our things carefully, just in case we found a way to return, and we agreed to explore ways to somehow return to do this again.

We received a reminder of the reality of 9/11 just before we returned to American, when we saw armed *carabinieri* patrolling the Milan airport before our flight home, and the heightened security led to an interesting up-close encounter with these stylish and well-armed officers. Because our suitcases were packed to the gills with our belongings, I had to carry on a heavy winter jacket, but I was also carrying a small suitcase, a computer case and a pillow. I put the jacket on as I walked through the Malpensa airport because I had too many things to carry comfortably—and the police logically thought it looked suspicious for a man to be wearing a heavy jacket in early July. Suddenly I was surrounded by three officers who wanted to know what I had under the jacket.

Fortunately by this time I could speak Italian well enough to explain my situation, and they let me pass. I was already sweating enough from the warmth; the added anxiety of my close encounter with the law convinced me to keep my jacket off during the rest of my wait in the airport.

As for Suzye and Lindsey, when they returned to the states to a happy reunion with their friends, they found that something had changed—they had—and for the better. They found their eyes had been opened by their exposure to Italy, Slovenia, Austria, Germany, England and France. Suddenly the social world of Gig Harbor seemed small and their friends' attitudes limited, provincial and focused on appearances and trivial matters.

As we worked together in our road maintenance business that summer, I asked them how their attitudes about our Italian adventure had changed over time.

"After I got back, I couldn't relate to my friends as much anymore," Lindsey said. "I'd seen so much of the world and had new dreams and things that I wanted to do, so I felt different. Before I was a very typical Gig Harbor teenage girl, with a much smaller perspective. I'm so glad that we went, because we learned how to travel, and it opened up my eyes to the world. We learned how to talk to people that we didn't always have a lot in common with."

When I reminded Suzye how she had cried and complained while in Italy, she said, "That's not the part I remember anymore. Looking back, I just remember all the good stuff, and I'm so glad I went. I came back all fit and tan, and I had so much fun going out with Erica."

I also overheard Suzye and Lindsey telling people how thankful they were that we had taken them to Italy. Had they changed their opinion by the end of our time there, or was it after we returned?

"Probably not until after I came back," Suzye said. "I wouldn't have admitted it to you there."

I wondered if their parents' unilateral decision to move to Italy had damaged the parent-child relationship. Had they been angry, and did this contribute to some of their acts of rebellion? No, they said, they were just going through some of the typical teen rites of passage at the time.

"I definitely wasn't angry," Lindsey said. "I thought you were really brave, because you didn't have a job. You had a dream and you just decided to follow it. Moving your whole family and your two angsty teenage daughters and not having a clear plan was really brave. I was very proud of you guys, that you managed it.

"Suzye and I got in kind of a strange mental stage . . . we weren't fully living in the present. We were sort of collecting experiences so we could bring that back to our lives in America instead of just enjoying the lives we had in Italy. We would go shopping a lot and buy clothes and not really wear them there but just plan to bring them home so we could wear them at home. That's no way to live. I really regret that a lot, because I think my life in Italy was way more interesting that it is back home. I thought that I was going to miss my friends. It wasn't really until I got back that I realized I didn't miss anything. Then I fully appreciated the fact that I had gone to Italy. I grew up a lot. It definitely changed my life. It woke me up to the world."

When we came home, I had changed, too, and I no longer wanted to return to my old teaching position. For twenty-two years, I had poured all my effort and passion into my job, especially the student newspaper, but the last two years I had begun to sense the fire burning down just a little. It was a job that took tremendous commitment to do well, and I didn't want to sell my students short by being less than 100 percent enthusiastic. Also, I had broadened my own interests, and my passion for Italy had come to full flame. Though I could have had my old position back, I changed to a job teaching science and technology to ninth graders at a junior high school. And for the first time, I began to research retirement benefits, trying to figure out a way to retire early.

My new teaching job proved enjoyable, and the best part: It no longer consumed me the way my journalism assignment had done. I found time to pursue other interests. I self-published my children's book (under the pen name Mabel

Barr), I built a new house as an investment and source of rental income, I expanded the activities of my summer business, and I developed a new hobby, genealogy. I also continued to explore how I could fulfill my dream of going back to Italy for another extended stay, without being burdened with the need to work while living there.

Spending summers in Italy was not a consideration for us. It is too crowded with tourists and much too hot. That, and the money I earned in the summer was an essential part of my plan for early retirement. Lucy and I did travel to Italy nearly every spring vacation, though, going to a different area of the country each year with one question burning in the background: Where would be the ideal place to live when we retired? Nearly eight years of scheming, investing, saving and working ten hours a day each summer later, we began living our Italian dream once more. And that's a story for another day.

Postscript: Chasing the elusive magical elf called Permesso di Soggiorno

I n writing about my *permesso* experiences, I wondered how the process may have changed in the ensuing years. I found that in 2007, the procedures were altered slightly—I'd almost say simplified, but they may actually have been made more complicated. Instead of starting out at the Questura, now one must start at the post office—not just any post office but one that has a *sportello amico*, a friend window. Theoretically, this should be an improvement, because the lines at the post offices are somewhat shorter than those at the Questura, but there are different procedures to learn when queuing in a post office line. Another thing that sounds better about the new procedure is that after a person correctly submits all forms to the post office, he is given an actual appointment at the Questura. However, from all that I have read, the actual hour of the appointment is meaningless, as one still must wait in the Questura line based on arrival time, not appointment time.

I also found an online account from 2009 that had me rolling on the floor. It was written by Nathan Randall in his blog *The adventures of Nataniele Randaglio-Part 2*, dated December 1, 2009. Nate has kindly granted me permission to reprint his work here.

Here's what I've had to go through in order to get my *permesso di soggiorno*—a permit of stay, of sorts, that declares my presence in Italy completely legit. The *permesso*, here, is a nebulous concept. It's unclear who needs it, how to get it, what it looks like, even. Some say it's a paper document, others insist it's more of a plastic card, and even others claim it to be a magical Italian elf that follows you around assuring your legality via interpretive song and dance to those who doubt it.

Step 1: Go to the post office and pick up the application. To do this, you must first wait in line, which you'll do politely for five and a half minutes, unsure of where the line begins or ends, before remembering that the post offices in Italy require you to push a button on a machine near the doorway that gives you a paper ticket identifying, officially, your place among the other people in line. Actually, a very nice system that helps you avoid those awkward "who got here first?" interactions with strangers. The funny thing, you'll notice, is that nobody bothers to sit down in the provided chairs to wait their turn. People, it seems, are so used to fighting for spots in such lines that they'll stand in the post office lobby, clutching their paper tickets with white, angry knuckles and staring anxiously at the neon numbers counting upwards on the NBA-scoreboard-style counter in the center of the office. When it's finally your turn, you'll go to the postal worker and ask for the application, only to learn that there are, in fact, several buttons on that paper ticket emitting machine near the doorway, and that you pushed the wrong one and must redo the process. On try number two, you will get it right, go to a different window, and finally receive the documents to proceed.

Step 2: Reading the documents back at school, you'll see that one of them requires a *marca da bollo*. Having heard stories from permesso applicants of years past, you'll already know that a *marca da bollo* is an official, government-issued stamp that you must purchase not at the post office, where you foolishly assume you would get an official, government-issued stamp, but in fact at one of the tobacco distributors in town. Proud of yourself for being so *permesso* savvy, you'll go straight to the tobacco distributor and spend $14.92 on your very own *marca da bollo*.

Step 3: Once finished filling out the application forms in either black or blue pen, you'll go to the photocopy room at school to make the as-requested photocopies of your official documents, including, reasonably enough, your passport, which you'll wisely bring to school with you that morning. Just as you did when you applied for your visa back in the states, you'll photocopy all of the passport's relevant pages—that is, the front page with your name and personal information, the page with your visa, and the page with your entrance stamp.

Step 4: All in the same day, you'll return to the post office, convinced that you'll impress the postal workers with your dedication to immigration regulations. You'll push the right button on your first try, wait (on foot, of course) with everybody else, stare at the NBA-scoreboard-style counter until it's your turn and then present both yourself and your well-organized folder of documents to the postal worker. When she gets to your passport photocopies, you'll mentally notice that you did a really great job choosing an appropriate level of photocopy darkness. So content will you be with your artwork that you won't realize the postal worker is addressing you.

"Where are the rest of the passport photocopies," she'll be saying.

Finally coming to. "What do you mean?"

"You need to photocopy all of the pages."

"All of the pages?"

"Yes. All of the pages."

You'll chew on this for a second. "Even the blank ones at the end?"

"Yes. Of course. And the covers as well. Front and back."

Step 5: You'll return to the school photocopy room and make photocopies of all twenty-five pages of your passport and both covers, thanking to yourself that at least you have access to free photocopies.

Step 6: Tired of going to the post office in the city where you work, you'll take a train back to your host family's house and go to the post office in the city where you live, bringing your completed application, all of your photocopies, a new sense of purpose and a refusal to give in to the man. As it turns out, the people at this post office will be much friendlier, and after demonstrating your expertise with the ticket emitting button machine, you'll race through the rest of the process and be granted your first official *permesso* appointment—scheduled for 8:46 a.m. (yes, 8:46 a.m.)--at the Questura in the province's capital. In your case, this capital will be located about 40 kilometers away, but you'll be lucky because your appointment will be scheduled for the one day of the week that you don't have morning classes.

Step 7: Three weeks later, you'll hop on an early train to the province's capital and report to the Questura at 8:33 a.m. There, you'll find a cement lobby, empty of chairs but full of immigrants from all over the world funneling towards the glass doors leading into the immigration office. And this time there will be no ticket emitting button machine, so you'll have to employ all the skills you learned in middle school lacrosse practices in order to stay on your feet and maintain your ground. Painstakingly slowly, you'll nudge your way, with the rest of the crowd, towards the tip of the funnel. After an hour of waiting, and gently pushing, and waiting some more, you'll be at the front of the line, and enter the glass doors. There, you'll have a young immigration officer so fascinated by your American citizenship that he won't even look at the documents you've worked so hard to prepare, and which have been sent there from the post office you first went to. Rather, he'll accept them all, rush you through the fingerprinting process (yes, you'll get fingerprinted), congratulate you on making it through the first step without any hitches and then give you another appointment for three weeks later, once again at the Questura in the capital of your province. Confused, you'll say: "Wait. But... sir... you just fingerprinted me. Why do I need to come back for more fingerprints? I'll have to miss school . . . and take another train . . . and waste . . . . I mean . . . use, not waste, use, an entire day. Can't I do them now?"

And he'll say: "No. I'm sorry. Different machine, different fingerprints. Be sure not to miss your appointment."

Step 8: Defeated, you'll get a gelato in an attempt to cheer yourself up. (It'll work pretty well.)

Step 9: Three weeks later, you'll return to the capital of your province. This time, you'll get there two hours early and be the first in line. You'll take more fingerprints, as well as full-fledged palm and hand prints, before being congratulated on having completed the second stage of your *permesso di soggiorno*. You won't bother telling the fingerprint technician that this is, in fact, the ninth stage. Instead, you'll thank him politely, and leave. You'll note that even if you'd had all of the documents that second time you went to the post office, you still would have needed to make six different trips in order to complete the process. The first, to pick up the application. The second to purchase the *marca da bollo* from the *tabacchiao*. The third to submit everything to the post office. The fourth to go to the Questura to go over (for a second time) your documents, and then conduct fingerprints. The fifth time to return to the Questura for more finger and hand prints. And the sixth time to pick the finished document up.

Step 10: You'll go back to your home and blog about the experience so that your friends and family can understand how much incentive the system gives you to seeing these bureaucratic processes through.

Nate's step 10 is optional, of course, but I'm glad he did it, because his experiences and writing really cracked me up. In a later blog, he took one more trip to the Questura and actually picked up his *permesso*, which was not a magical elf but actually a plastic card, though by this time it was almost time for him to return to the U.S.

In defense of the system, I found another website that said the fingerprinting process was now done in one appointment, and the post office no longer requires that blank pages of the passport be copied. The site also says that you don't need to wait in line for the packet. You just go to the counter and ask for "*il kit del permesso di soggiorno*" for EU citizens. On the downside, for services rendered, the post office also requires an administrative fee of 27.50 euro, which is in addition to the 14.62 euro *marca da bollo* tax and the 30 euro Ministry of

Finance charge. However, there are now web sites providing more step-by-step directions than were available for me and Nate.

To follow more of our adventures, you can read our blog: <u>Living (with) Abroad in Tuscany</u>. I'd also really appreciate your leaving an honest book review on the Amazon or Goodreads websites.

Grazie

Thanks to Lucy, the most supportive, encouraging and helpful wife a man could hope to have, and to Suzye and Lindsey for interrupting their lives to help me follow my dream—and then to all three for helping me put together our memories of that eventful year. Another big thanks to my editor, Lizzie Harwood, whose suggestions made this book many times better than it was before I sent it to her. I also greatly appreciate the help of beta readers Nancy Jenkins Mammi, Lindsey Spadoni, Greg Spadoni and Linda Spadoni, and the advice of author E.C. Murray. The fine cover art is the work of Banashree Das, with some creative suggestions from Nick Goettling. The rest of the cover was crafted by Jesh Designs.

An interview with Paul Spadoni.

So, who is Paul Spadoni, really?

Like most people, I'm full of contradictions. I'm an introvert who admires extroverts. I'm quiet, maybe even shy, but I have no fear of speaking to large crowds. Most of my friends would say I'm conservative in my life views, but I like to take risks in certain areas of my life, which surprises people. My life has been shaped by my personal faith in God, but I don't wear my faith on my shirtsleeves. I grew up very proud of my Italian-American heritage and have always had an appreciation for the sacrifices made by my parents, grandparents—all my ancestors, really—to give me a better life.

Actually, I just meant to ask, what is your occupation?

Oh, of course. Well, I usually need some context to answer that question. If it's in relation to my construction work, I'm the owner and operator of a road repair business. By education, I am either a journalist or a teacher. I've been trained for both and I've spent many years doing both. In fact, for twenty-one years, I was actually a teacher of journalism. But now that I'm retired from teaching and only work five months a year in my business, when my friends in Italy ask me during one of my seven free months, I might say I am *impensionato*, retired. Now that I've published two books, I sometimes say I'm an author. So it depends on who's asking and how I feel at the moment.

So, do you prefer living in America or in Italy?

All of the above. We live in Italy about four months a year and in America the rest of the time. We have homes in both places, and it works out just perfectly. We usually live in Italy in late winter and early spring, and then again for about a month in the fall. This takes advantage of the moderate weather in Italy during these seasons, and then the beautiful summers of the Pacific Northwest. Our immediate family is in the States, and that's a strong draw to be there for the greater part of the year, and especially during the winter holidays. After a few months in one country, we start yearning for the other again, so going back and forth leaves us always with something fun to look forward to.

What's next for you? Do you have any other books in your head?

I suppose I should write about our explorations in Tuscany and how we ended up finding hundreds of relatives—some dead, some alive—and then buying a house there. I'd also love to write about my years as a high school journalism teacher. But writing and publishing is a heck of a lot of work. Still I have no doubt I will write more.

Made in the USA
San Bernardino, CA
30 July 2017